Dwelling in a Strange Land

John Holdsworth was born in Yorkshire but has spent all his adult life as an ordained Anglican minister in Wales. Alongside his service in parishes throughout South Wales, he spent ten years as a TV presenter with HTV Wales, and still broadcasts frequently. Until recently he was Principal of St Michael's Theological College in Llandaff, Cardiff, and Dean of the Faculty of Theology at Cardiff University. He is currently Archdeacon of St David's. John is married with two grown up children, and lives in Pembrokeshire.

Dwelling in a Strange Land

Exile in the Bible and in the Church

John Holdsworth

CANTERBURY
PRESS
Norwich

© John Holdsworth 2003

First published in 2003 by the Canterbury Press Norwich
(a publishing imprint of Hymns Ancient &
Modern Limited, a registered charity)
St Mary's Works, St Mary's Plain,
Norwich, Norfolk, NR3 3BH

www.scm-canterburypress.co.uk

British Library Cataloguing in Publication data

A catalogue record for this book is available
from the British Library

ISBN 1-85311-563-0

Typeset by Regent Typesetting, London
Printed and bound by
Bookmarque Ltd, Croydon, Surrey

Contents

Acknowledgements

The book was written during a period of sabbatical leave from my job as Principal of St Michael's Theological College in Llandaff Cardiff. I am grateful to the Trustees for their support in the project and particularly to the Bishop of Llandaff, now Archbishop, for his practical help. The Isla Johnson Trust provided some of the funds which enabled me to spend the sabbatical in New Zealand as the guest of St John's Theological College in Auckland. I am particularly grateful to the staff there for their stimulus and hospitality and particularly to the Principal John Wright for his gracious welcome. The facilities of the Kinder Library and the personal interest of Assistant Librarian Helen Greenwood made the task particularly pleasant. Of course the scheme would never have got off the ground without the enthusiastic support of Archbishop Rowan Williams, whose continuing interest has been invaluable. I am grateful also to Bishop Peter Atkins and Professor Stephen Pattison for their comments on the finished script. The stimulus of generations of students and invaluable discussions and conversations with colleagues have shaped the material, but of course I take responsibility for its shortcomings despite all that. The presence of my wife, and for a short time, my daughter, helped me to appreciate

settledness in the midst of restlessness, and the book is
dedicated to them both.

To Sue and Zoë
gyda chariad

Introduction

For myself, I have never had much time for the kind of Introduction that demands to be read. I much prefer the kind of book, which, like a novel, introduces itself and its plot at its own pace and within the text, without need for some prior apology. That is the kind of book that I have written. However, when a book is advertised specifically as a Lent book it is perhaps fitting to explain why that title might be appropriate. This book is designed as a resource for those who want to question, want to learn, want to be stimulated, want to make new connections and want, above all, to make some sense of what it might mean to be a Christian in the world today. All these, I take it, are connected with the proper observance of Lent. It is specifically designed for those who want to reflect. It is based on an understanding that theology is not a set of given principles, axioms and propositions which need to be learned and perhaps adapted. Rather, theology is what emerges from a conversation, or perhaps even a collision, between Christian traditions on the one hand and the reader's context in the contemporary world on the other. Reflection on this understanding is the task of enabling that conversation to happen.

The book's division into nine chapters might be helpful to those who wish to use it as a group resource, covering the Lent and pre-Lent period. But it need not be used in that way. It can equally well be read straight through, and by individuals, at any time. A feature of the presentation of the book is its juxtaposition of text and exercises. Some may wonder why such exercises have not been collected together at the end of each chapter. The arrangement is deliberate. If the book is based on an understanding that theology is generated by reflection, then the exercises give opportunity for that, enabling text, tradition and context to be brought together in a progressive way which makes the reader more of a participant than an observer. The exercises can be ignored but the whole project will be more useful and much more fun if they are not. In any case the chapters should be read sequentially. This is not a book to dip into. It presents a developing argument. Though some prior knowledge of the Bible and some experience of a faith community would be an advantage, all you really need to begin to engage with this book is curiosity.

John Holdsworth
Steynton
Feast of St Mary Magdalene

I

Ground Zero

Introduction

Once upon a time there was a nation that considered itself particularly favoured. The people of the nation lived in a land that had rich natural resources, and agricultural lands sufficient to support them. They didn't want to live anywhere else. They had not always lived in the land. The first people who arrived had a difficult journey as they fled oppression and religious persecution. When they reached the land it was already inhabited by other people from other nations or tribes but they overcame them by force. Stories about those heroic times had become part of the folklore of the people. Over time they settled and developed the land. They had a series of laws, which they considered to be before their time. Those enlightened laws became part of the special identity of the people.

They were a religious people who believed in one God, and as their prosperity increased, they believed they had been specially blessed. There were voices, from time to time, that warned the people that their behaviour was not always at one with their religious profession, but they were largely ignored. The leaders of the people had religious advisers who were convinced that God had a special plan for the nation. They were convinced that the values identified with this nation were the ones that God wanted to see throughout the world, and that the nation had a special role in helping to bring this about, by force if necessary. Everyone believed that this state of secure happiness would continue for ever. Then one day something terrible happened; something that cast doubt on all their assumptions; something of such significance that it raised new and fundamental questions, and caused the people to look again at their beliefs. The nation was called America, and the date was September 11, 2001.

Some thousands of years earlier we have records of another story that bears strong resemblance to that one. This too is a story about a nation which considered itself specially favoured and blessed. It reckoned to have a special relationship with its God who was considered a cut above all others. The practical effects of this relationship were that the people who had once been oppressed slaves now had a land of their own. They had a series of laws which they considered to be before their time and which gave shape and identity to their society. They believed that the special relationship guaranteed them tenure to the land, and guaranteed that they would have progeny to be its future inhabitants. Special religious advisers, largely uncritically supportive, called court prophets, were from time to time consulted about political decisions, but increasingly a group of religious spokesmen emerged, claiming to speak on behalf of God himself, who questioned both the lifestyle and the political direction and leadership of the nation. They were largely ignored. And then something terrible happened; something that cast doubt on all the nation's assumptions; something of such significance that it raised new and fundamental questions, and caused the people to look again at their beliefs. The year was 597 BCE. This time the nation was called Judah, and the catastrophe came to be called the Exile.

Reflection on Experience

What does the term 'exile' mean to you? Write down the names of any groups or individuals you might consider to be in exile today of which you have heard. The list might include, for example:

- Refugees of various kinds;
- Individuals who have been expelled from their native land because of something they've written or said;
- People who have moved from their native land to be with their family or to do a specific job.

If you are doing this as a group exercise, compare your lists. What do the people on your lists have in common? What is the difference between an exile, an ex-pat and a tourist/traveller? Do you know any exiles? Might it be possible to speak to them about what it feels like to be an exile?

The Exile

The beginning of the Exile is described in stark historical style in 2 Kings, chapters 24 and 25. A more compelling and human account of the events, the political manoeuverings, and the sheer terror in the face of the enormity of this act is to be found throughout the book of the prophet Jeremiah (for a flavour, see for example 8:18 – 9:11). What happened, according to these accounts, is that a foreign power successfully conquered Jerusalem and took away, on two separate occasions, over a ten-year period, anyone who was anyone, to captivity in Babylon. Certainly all the movers and shakers were taken: civil servants, religious and political figures, members of the royal family along with what we might now call the middle classes and a substantial number of artisans. Those who were not brutally killed were shipped off on the long march to a foreign land. Just a token number of the poorest people – the kind of people who always seem largely unaffected by political change because they have little vested in any particular system – were left to be vinedressers and tillers of the soil (2 Kings 25:12). The effect was that all the nation's hopes and dreams were in tatters. The things they had been most certain about had been called into question. The things that had given them distinctive identity were destroyed. Jerusalem itself, and its temple, a monument in stone to the belief system that controlled the nation, was now just rubble; sixth-century ground zero. They even remembered the date.

Described like that, these two events seem tantalizingly similar – similar enough, perhaps, to suggest that it might even be possible to interpret the latter, September 11, in the light of the Old Testament response to Exile; or that at the very least, a consideration of that response might provide a fruitful engine for reflection. And if that is so, what other events or experiences might be considered in this way with similar profit? What of the Holocaust, the enslavement of millions of Africans in the seventeenth and eighteenth centuries, the massacres in Rwanda or Bosnia in more recent history; the experience of being a refugee from war or famine which has characterized many peoples, or the experience of people like the Kurds or Palestinians who have had to flee their native land when it was conquered by others, but who retain a dream of its restoration. And need we stop at national historical events of this kind? What of the huge personal tragedies which beset most of us at some time, upsetting the equilibrium of our lives, threatening their foundations and scattering their landmarks? In an increasingly mobile society in the West, many of us feel displaced, without a real home and identity. Is this, also, the kind of experience for which the Exile might provide a reflective tool? Or are we asking too much of a potential paradigm which many scholars would say is itself too shrouded in mystery anyway to be of help?

Starting Points

For me there are two reasons for embarking on this book. The first was triggered for me by September 11. As we shall see there is an increasing number of scholars who want to say that the theme of exile has something to teach us today about appropriate forms of church life. They urge us to take seriously the designation of the church as a group of exiles, presupposed in the word 'parish' which derives from the Greek word for 'resident aliens', *paroikia*. This word is sometimes paired in the Bible with another, *parepidemoi*, meaning sojourners or exiles, (as at 1 Peter 1:1). But I am not convinced that they are drawing the right conclusions. The Old Testament writers bear witness to a people whose argument is not so much with Babylon as with God himself. Before September 11 it may have been natural to think about the church's exile in terms of its difference from sur-rounding culture, and so to urge the church to a new sense of its distinctive identity. But from September 12 onwards that will not do. We have had a stark reminder that the crux of exile is not living in a foreign place. It is the sense of abandonment that comes from seeing one's familiar landmarks of meaning, and perhaps even their icons, the structures and institutions that embody them, destroyed. If it was right to make the connection between the Twin Towers atrocity and the Old Testament Exile in the way we did in the opening paragraphs then the American people will have entered an exile without ever leaving home. They will have to rethink things they thought were settled and resolved for all time. And I want to look at how the Old Testament deals with that, and what kind of church that whole process might point us towards.

The second reason for writing is about Old Testament study itself. In the seminary and university where I work, I am required to teach courses on the Old Testament to a variety of students. Some of them have had little exposure to communities of faith and their texts. Others, through long and bored acquaintance, have long since written off the Old Testament; whilst yet others struggle against seemingly insuperable odds to find some point of access to, or some kind of handle on, this daunting and varied body of writings. I have a passion to describe these texts in a way that will be both interesting and compelling. When I was a student, an interest in the Old Testament was viewed with suspicion. Each scholar who wrote about this part of the Bible seemed to be vying with his (usually his) immediate predecessors to be more boring and esoteric than they. It was impossible to read works of scholarship without exceptional eyesight, boundless stamina and a working knowledge of the German language. To admit to an interest in the Old Testament was tantamount to confessing that one was a train spotter and collector of stamps. And certainly any suggestion that it was the Old Testament which might provide a central interpretative idea for contemporary faith would have been thought novel to say the least. But over the last thirty years or so all that has changed.

It probably began with those liberation theologians who saw, in the account of the Exodus from slavery to settlement in the promised land, a new model, a new way, a new paradigm for interpreting the lot of those who today could be said to live as oppressed slaves. The words of Exodus 2:23f. seemed to connect in a new and vital way with those who today groan under their slavery and cry out. They seemed to give assurance that God hears the

poor, the underclass. That in turn prompted new sociolog-
ical interest in the Old Testament. For years scholars had
written as if the only thing that mattered about the people
of Israel was their faith, and that they lived their lives in
some kind of religious cocoon unconcerned about the
practical things of life which consume people like us. Now
we were able to see them in some kind of social context and
to connect with their class struggles and their problems
with authority and power. The tools of sociology applied to
the Bible led to conclusions or hypotheses greatly at odds
with the comfortable shared assumptions of an earlier age
of scholarship. Had the conquest of Canaan happened
exactly as set out in the book of Joshua? Were we really to
accept the concept of ancient Israel as historically accurate?
These were heady times.

Suddenly Old Testament scholars discovered how to
write in a way that could capture the imagination of
non-specialists. Books with inviting titles such as *Exquisite
Desire*, complete with lurid cover illustrations, tempt
potential readers to a treatment of the theme of the erotic.
Other books have catchy controversial titles like *Propa-
ganda and Subversion in the Old Testament* or *The Inven-
tion of Ancient Israel*. And a great deal of this new vigour
coincides with a growing conviction that the Exile, rather
than the Exodus, is the key event which connects the varied
elements of the Old Testament. Perhaps at last we have a
handle, and more than that, a handle which can enable
us to make links between these ancient documents and
contemporary experience.

And that matters to me as well, for in addition to being a
teacher, I am a preacher, pastor and theologian. As such, I
have a role with regard to the community of faith which
includes helping the interaction between the community's
context, on the one hand, and the Bible on the other, and to
allow each to react with the other in a way that has the
potential to transform both. When Christians learn about

the biblical Exile, it is my experience that they are better equipped to get on with the business of transforming the world. When people bring their own experience of exile to bear on the text, it seems that this can open up a whole new realm of understanding for them, which in turn can deepen faith and commitment. In short, the Old Testament has, for me, become a series of writings connected by the theme of exile. In turn those writings have become a new resource for understanding both religion and the world, and I want to share this approach more widely.

Introducing the Old Testament

How would you begin to introduce the Old Testament to people who had never read it? One possibility would be to outline the different kinds of material that it contains. So we may concentrate on different literary genres: poetry, drama, saga and so on. Or we might perhaps describe it under the three headings which reflect its Jewish origins: Law, Prophets and Writings, and say something briefly about each of these subdivisions and the books they contain. Or again we might begin with a vivid picture of the Old Testament world, hoping to make the point that the books can only be fully understood in their historic, social and cultural context.

This last would be the trickiest of the three because it makes the most assumptions. It assumes, for example, that we can in fact reconstruct a history of the times described in the Bible. Scholars are increasingly wary about such an assumption, particularly as for the most part that history can only be reconstructed from biblical sources. And that in turn assumes perhaps that the biblical accounts were meant to be read as offering an accurate account of history. Moreover, insights from sociology have warned us that there is no such thing as disinterested history. Histories are always written from a point of view, and if we accept the point of view of one author we might get a distorted view of what really happened. Take a simple example. An anti-government protest march is organized in the capital. Invariably the numbers attending will be inflated by those newspapers supporting the cause, and underestimated by those newspapers supporting the government. The way the story is reported will aim either to recruit more converts to the cause by giving the impression that the marchers speak for a vast constituency, or to stifle protest by claiming that they are a small minority of zealous fanatics. Even the choice of photographs will support whichever argument is being made. And that is just what each 'report' is – an argument. No one can surely claim that texts sacred to millions of people for thousands of years are bland objective reports. They aim to convince us of something and we have to be aware of that as we read them as history.

Scholars also distinguish between two kinds of historical enquiry. On the one hand there is the history of events. Things happen. On the other there is the history of the texts that describe them. When were they written and why? Did they develop and were they altered? The historian works with critical tools which seek to throw light on these questions and a great deal of biblical scholarship has worked on the same principles. By trying to discern how texts developed, scholars have tried to assemble a picture of what actually happened. However, the events of history can be used in a different way, a way which is best accessed by scholars of literature rather than history. For example the English king Richard II reigned from 1377 to 1399. Long after Richard's time, in 1596, William Shakespeare published a play called *Richard II*, but his reason for doing so, and the particular points he wanted to emphasize are actually dictated by the concerns and politics of Shakespeare's own time. Christopher Marlowe's play *Edward II* published in 1594, is another attempt to discuss controversial current issues against the backcloth of the life of a long-dead king. This time it may have less to do with politics than with the issue of homosexuality. Historians still have a part to play in helping scholars of literature know how best to interpret *Richard II* or *Edward II* by enabling them to understand the social context of late sixteenth-century society. In turn, scholars of literature may even help to throw light on that context as a result of their study of the text. This interaction is not controversial because we know that *Richard II* and *Edward II* are historical plays. But imagine the confusion if we did not. Likewise, a great deal of scholarly activity is deployed today in arguing the respective merits of Exodus over against the biblical account of Exodus, and even Ancient Israel over against the biblical concept, 'Ancient Israel'.

Unravelling Texts with Suspicion

People called 'source critics' and 'form critics' have spent long years in the last century and before, trying to unravel Old Testament texts using the tools and presuppositions of historical criticism. But it is commonplace now to find scholars arguing that the agendas of the writers and the history of the times in which they wrote are going to be equally important as the 'history' of the events they describe, if we are to get to the bottom of our quest for truth. Again, though, we can only guess at what those agendas might be, often helped by the tools of another discipline, sociology.

One way of reading, which derives from the insights of sociology, is called the 'hermeneutic of suspicion'. This means that we read the texts, not naively, but with a view to identifying the point of view of the writer, by asking questions like: In whose interest is this account written? Whose interests are not served or whose voice is not heard? Might the account be an attempt to justify the position of the powerful at the expense of the poor? or a setting out of a male agenda? or an apologia for a party view about politics or religion?

Reflection on Text

If you're feeling brave you might like to try this exercise to get the feel of how the 'hermeneutic of suspicion' works. Look at the list of the Ten Commandments in Exodus 20:3–17. Now ask yourself, in whose interest are these commandments written? Who gains most by having laws like this? Is it, for example:

- The young or the old?
- Those with property or those without ?
- City dwellers or those who live in the country?

One writer who commends this exercise, reaches the conclusion that the commandments will favour most, 'a balding Israelite urban male with a mid-life crisis and a weight problem, in danger of losing his faith'.[1] What do you think of that judgement?

With regard to the Old Testament the picture is more fascinating and complicated even than this, because sometimes we have more than one account of events. The books from Joshua through to 2 Kings contain a history of Israel outlining the rise and fall of the monarchy from Israel's beginnings as a nation through to the Exile. Exactly the same story is told in 1 and 2 Chronicles but in a completely different way and reaching different conclusions about the lessons to be drawn from it all. Sometimes different writers rework old materials and place them in a new framework.

One of the most famous conclusions of the work of the source critics, for example, is that the first five books of the Old Testament actually contain material from four distinct periods of Israelite history, each successive contribution subtly changing the conclusions the reader might reach about the origins of Israel. One of the really interesting questions to ask as each stage of tradition is unravelled is: Why was a further edition necessary? What prompted it and how does it help the theme develop?

But even if we could write a history of Israel which has academic integrity, how would that help us? Or if we could describe the literary nature of its contents with complete confidence what would we have gained? It might be interesting to do so were we students of ancient history or culture, but what if we happen to be theologians? Communities of faith do not read these documents because they want to find out what really happened thousands of years ago. They read them in order to inform faith in the present. They want to know what we can learn about God in all this. They want to know not so much what happened, but rather why that was thought to be significant. Why did it matter, and why should it matter today? Attempting to introduce the Old Testament by outlining a history of the times might then not only seriously distort the message, but might also present it in a way which is entirely irrelevant to those who want to find answers to questions of meaning and purpose. What we shall want to know is what kinds of event prompted fundamental rethinks and rewrites.

Paradise Lost

What might this mean in practice as we seek to understand the meaning of the Old Testament? It might mean that we do not ask questions such as: Did the Exodus or the Conquest happen in exactly the ways set out in the texts? but rather questions such as: Why did writers at a particular time believe that by telling the story in a particular way they were answering the questions that were being raised by their own generation? And it is increasingly the conviction of scholars that the writings of the Old Testament were in a large part designed to answer questions raised by the Exile. Our introduction to the Old Testament might therefore more usefully begin by looking at what those questions were, and how the texts connect with them.

It is difficult to overestimate the importance of the Exile for the people of Israel. On the basis of what we now call the Sinai Covenant (set out in the Old Testament at, for example Exodus 20–23), the special relationship between God and the people, with its promises and obligations on both sides, was spelled out. According to ancient and mostly oral traditions, the giving of this Covenant was itself part of a process which went back into the mists of time at least as far as Abraham, whose name means 'father of a nation'. God's part of the deal involved his making three promises. First, Israel would have a land of its own. Second, the people of Israel would have descendants, so safeguarding the continuation of the nation for perpetuity. And third, God would always have a special relationship with them: they would be his people and he would be their God. This relationship is often spelled out in very warm, tender and affectionate terms. God is to be like a father to a son, like a husband to a wife. This was the basis on which Israel as a nation was built. These were the marks of its distinctive identity of which it was so proud. Questions of meaning and purpose in life were explored against the background of these promises.

Imagine then what the Exile represented. The promise of land seemed to have come to nothing, since the people were being transported elsewhere, probably never to return. The promise of progeny looked increasingly fragile, since as time went on the likelihood would be that people from

Israel, Judeans as they were now called, would marry foreigners. A people without a land have little chance of maintaining their identity to start with, but once they break ethnic ranks the problem is even worse. And above all, what about the promise that God would have a special relationship that involved some kind of protection? Clearly that was shot to pieces. Everything therefore that these people had relied on to provide them with distinctive identity and access to meaning had been destroyed. It was their September 11, their first holocaust.

Reflection on Experience

Where were you when you heard the news about September 11, 2001? Can you remember your first feelings, and the first questions you had? Do you see any similarities between that event and what we have described as the Old Testament Exile? Have a look back at the opening paragraphs of this chapter then make a two-column list setting out the similarities as you see them. You might like to do the same thing setting out differences. If you are doing this as a group activity see how your results compare with others. Is there a common view?

Responses

In such situations there are two kinds of response which we can recognize from more contemporary events. On the one hand there are those who ask: How could God let this happen? This can often lead to a further reflective question, what have we done to deserve this? On the other, there are those who perhaps more radically or cynically take the events as proof that there never was an agreement, never was a Covenant, perhaps never was a God, and that the whole thing was a cruel delusion. So the first priority for those who remain within the community of faith is to find ways of countering the latter views and exploring the former questions by looking back and re-examining the story. In all probability, this is how the Old Testament as we know it, began.

We have already noted that source critics tell us four distinct traditions can be discerned within the first five books of the Bible – the Pentateuch. These are the books which tell the story of Israel's origins, and especially of the relationship between God and Israel. One of these traditions probably dates from the time when Israel had a king and all seemed well. Because the author of this source usually uses the name Yahweh or in Old English, Jehovah, we usually call the source 'J'. This is an optimistic account which sees a close relationship between God and his creation. Genesis 2:4ff. is a good example of this source. Man is the first and foremost creature in the world. He has dominion over everything else. He even names the animals. Moreover he can chat with God in the garden of Eden in a very intimate way, in the middle of the afternoon.

Reflection on Text

Read **Genesis 2:4–24**, then read **Genesis 1:1 – 2:3**. Note any different things they have to say about the relationship of:

- Man and woman,
- Humankind and the rest of creation,
- Humankind and God.

Which of the two accounts would you prefer if you:

• Were a member of a green party?
• Were a feminist?
• Were writing a liturgy or piece of music to celebrate 'creation'?

What does this tell you about the different styles and agendas of these different sources?

A couple of hundred years later and things are not looking quite so bright for Israel. The nation is threatened by powerful nations on its borders. We also see some evidence from biblical prophets of the eighth century like Amos and Hosea that at least some people from the religious community believed that the nation was threatened by moral corruption from within. The writings from this source, which from the term the author uses for God, Elohim, we know as 'E', show God as a more distant and in a sense more supernatural figure who communicates with his creation through dreams and visions rather than the friendly personal chat. At some stage these two traditions became combined.

Radicals

But the people who really got things moving, apparently, were those responsible for the third set of traditions. This was a radical group, very much in favour of reforms instigated by King Josiah (2 Kings 22). Their manifesto is to be found in the book of Deuteronomy and we know them as 'D'. They believed that religious life needed a shake up. From their perspective, religion had become completely marginal to the life of Israel, and was not regarded as something to be taken seriously. They saw the divorce between religion and morality as potentially disastrous for society, and wanted more control over what was actually taught and understood as the religion of Yahweh, the God of the Covenant. There were lots of outlying shrines in remote areas where religious rituals apparently had little distinctively Yahwistic about them. They had borrowed so much from their pagan neighbours that they were able to incorporate quite alien concepts, such as worship of the Queen of Heaven, into their religion. This rot had to stop. The Deuteronomistic (D) writers agreed that there should be a very few centres of religious excellence (perhaps even just one in Jerusalem) for public worship but that most teaching about religion should be in the home, focused on, for example, the Passover meal. They wanted a new emphasis on *rejoicing* in religion; a breaking down of some of the old boundaries between sacred and secular, and a new adherence to the Covenant. This group was influenced by the words of the eighth and seventh-century prophets. Jeremiah was in fact one of their number. Their theological statement is found in the book of Deuteronomy, but perhaps their biggest achievement was to integrate the teachings of the prophets and the traditions about Israel's origins through writing a history of early Israel, known to scholars as the 'Deuteronomistic history', including the books from Joshua through to 2 Kings.

We said earlier that all histories have an agenda. This D history is written, in the light of the impending Exile, precisely to answer the question, how could God let this happen? What did we do wrong? And the answer it commends is this: Israel was badly led by poor kings who did nothing to halt the slide away from the demands of the Covenant. The Exile is God's punishment for that. The one exception is King Josiah (for a glowing account of whose exploits see 2 Kings 22:1 – 23:30, especially 23:25) and by then it was all too late (2 Kings 23:26). So these writers made a big contribution to the beginnings of the Old Testament. They wrote Deuteronomy, putting some of the key elements of the Covenant in the new context, appending them to the existing traditions about the very early days. They wrote, or collected together the materials to present a complete history of Israel designed as an answer to the question: How could God let the Exile happen? And, as a group, they may well have been responsible for the collecting together of prophetic traditions from earlier centuries. They did their work at the very beginning of the Exile.

The Exile lasted for about fifty years until the Babylonian empire was taken over by that of Persia. Towards the end of this period new prophetic voices began to be heard. In exile the people had raised many new questions. We see some of this in the works of the prophet Ezekiel and parts of Isaiah, some of which we shall deal with in the next chapter, but as it became clear that the Exile would one day end, one pressing question was: How shall we be able to maintain our life of faith, now that so many things have changed, if we are able to return? Like any community that has undergone great trauma and now looks towards a better future recognizing its vulnerability, the Judeans or Jews as they now became, looked first to the things that had sustained and helped them during their captivity. Among those 'marks of identity' were the keeping of the Sabbath, male circumcision and increased dependence on a more institutional form of religion.

Priests and Pacifists

The fourth and final writers of the Pentateuch now added their own traditions and glosses to the existing combination. In so doing they shape the priorities of the whole five-book document for us. Because the authors of this final source are reckoned to come from within those priestly institutions which are part of the new understanding of religious life, we know this source as 'P'. A new account of creation (Genesis 1), now prefaces the Pentateuch, with a much more liturgical feel, a far more harmonious and

pacifist approach to society, a humbler place for humankind, and an account of why the Sabbath should be kept.
Other writers were busy penning a new history of Israel,
still using ancient traditions but presenting the material not
to answer the question: How could God let this happen?
but rather: How will God help us to survive? and: What is
to be the shape of the religious life in these new times? We
have this in our Bibles as 1 and 2 Chronicles, Nehemiah and
Ezra. Meanwhile other prophets like Haggai were inspiring
the people who returned to rebuild the temple. This was
writing that took place over a long period after the Exile,
giving ample opportunity for reflection. In these works the
kings and the establishment are no longer the problem.
Unlike the Deuteronomistic history, now it is precisely the
royal and priestly and civic institutions of Israel that will
be essential for survival. Whereas in 2 Samuel, David's
philandering with Bathsheba is set out in all its embarrass-
ing detail, in Chronicles it isn't mentioned at all, and in fact
David and Solomon are the great heroes.

Reflection on Text

Read **2 Samuel 11:1 – 12:31**. Now read how the
Chronicler deals with the same passage of history in
1 Chronicles 20:1–3. How does each of the writers
help to further his agenda?

What we see then is that the great trauma of the Exile,
potentially disastrous for the faith, identity and even
existence of Israel, actually becomes one of the most
creative periods in its theology with lots of new works
being written and older traditions collected. It is because of
this that we have an Old Testament at all.

The scholarship of previous generations enabled people

to think imaginatively about their faith in terms of the Exodus. That was a series of traditions which connected with an understanding of faith as an adventure; the community of God as a travelling pilgrim people; and the goal of religion as liberation. It was a way of reading the traditions which made the vocabulary of covenant the focus of religious obligation. New ways of reading the traditions, which favour the Exile as a dominant motif make none of that redundant. They do, though, offer us a new focus, and in a world which includes events such as those of September 11, they also give us a contemporary foothold in the interpretative business. They remind us that some events are so momentous and raise such enormous questions about meaning and purpose in life that they become landmarks in any history or biography; and by making connections between that and the Exile experience they help us both to make sense of our faith and to interpret our worlds. In the next chapter we shall see some of the implications of that reflection as we learn from the remaining books of the Old Testament how the Exile demanded that people begin to think the unthinkable about God.

2

September 12

Where Is God in All This?

What might it have been like on the Old Testament Exile
equivalent of September 12? Perhaps the analogy with
America begins to fall apart at this point. The options
which were open to the people of Israel in their weakness
are different from those available to the Americans. The
Israelites were not strong, could not rally round their
leader, had no institutions to depend on and were faced
with the prospect of extinction. They were utterly abandoned. The extent of that abandonment is conveyed in the
book of Lamentations. And yet the questions they faced
have a hauntingly modern feel. In sharp profile, and
prompted by their particular experience, are some of the
basic questions of the human condition, such as: What is
life all about? What is the meaning of it all? Where is God
in all this?

Reflection on Experience

Have you ever asked, where is God in all this? What
kind of times were they? Was the question asked
because of something happening on the world stage,

or was it something personal? What kind of response did you make to the question, and how were you helped in that by the Bible or other church resources? What proved most helpful? Has the question finally been resolved for you or do you still wonder . . . ?

The Protection Racket

The most fundamental issue to be faced is that here is the point where the old religion of Yahweh should have died off once and for all. That religion was based on belief in a God who cared specially for his people, guaranteed them a land and guaranteed them progeny. The events of the Exile could have been read as the end of Israel as a distinctive nation, and certainly as a people with a land. So what was left? What kind of special relationship allows the whole people to be taken into captivity by alien people with standards far removed from those of Israel and whose brutality is recorded in such events as the slaying of the sons of Zedekiah while he was forced to watch, only to have his own eyes put out before being taken in fetters to Babylon (2 Kings 25:7)? The prophet Habakkuk no doubt speaks for many when he says to God, in effect, we might be bad as a nation, but we're not as bad as those who you are allowing to conquer us: 'Why do you look on the treacherous, and are silent when the wicked swallow those more righteous than they?' (Habakkuk 2:13).

And for many people that was probably the last straw. I expect they lost faith. In any case events like these often throw into sharp focus the superficiality of what passes for religious faith. Some clearly think that it's all about protection. We see the frustration of Jeremiah when confronted with precisely this attitude by the people of Pathros. They tell him, all our misfortunes started when we ceased making offerings to the Queen of Heaven. We're not going to listen to you. We're going to start making our offerings again and perhaps all will be well (Jeremiah 44:15–18). There is a view of religion not unlike the gangster protection racket. In the movies, as long as you pay the dues to the right boss at the right time, your business will not be ransacked and your livelihood ruined. You pay protection money as an insurance. It all works tolerably well until, either the demands become too great, or else the protector ceases to be able to protect and you're turned over by a rival outfit. In the religious version, as long as humankind performs the right rituals and offers the right sacrifices with the holy man at the holy time in the holy place, then in return God will protect and keep the world safe. If he doesn't then you might as well make sacrifices to the Queen of Heaven to see if she can succeed where God failed. Individuals can be further assured by doing the right thing, the thing that God wants, and sticking to the moral rules. In just this way people are rewarded and the world is not only safe but fair as well. The problem with a protection racket view of religion is that it only works as long as God is a credible boss. Little wonder that Jeremiah and his friends, followers of Josiah's reforms, members of the D group, should want to spell out what their understanding of Covenant religion is. For them the protection racket view of religion is a hollow parody of their understanding of the religion of Yahweh based on relationship and trust, thanksgiving and celebration. So the book of Deuteronomy pays particular attention to the meaning of Covenant and the way that ritual is to be understood, taking care also to make connections between religion and ordinary life that will not allow religion to be treated as a hobby. They then proceed, in the D histories, the books from Joshua through to 2 Kings, to show how Israel has consistently failed to live up to, or even properly understand, faith. The D writers are saying in effect to that audience: The faith you lost was not authentic Yahwistic faith anyway. I expect that made them feel better.

Reflection on Text

Read **Jeremiah 44**, and try to imagine yourself as
Jeremiah. What is the most frustrating thing about
this situation for you? Now imagine yourself as one of
these refugees to Egypt. Put yourself in their shoes
and try to see things from their point of view. Do
any modern situations spring to mind as you read?
For a concise statement of the way the writers of
Deuteronomy see the issue read **Deuteronomy
4:25–31**.

Crossroads

But even for many of those whose view of religion was less
superficial, faith would not survive this experience. A faith
that is based on good people thanking God because they've
prospered has no answers at all in the face of an Exile.
At such times religious faith can seem to many people to
be empty, arid and naive, unable to cope with the awful
realities of life. There is a real fragility to faith in a loving
God, a faith which urges its adherents to neighbourly love
and care because that reflects this understanding of God, in
contexts of senseless brutality and apparently meaningless
tragedy. Responses to this are interesting. There is a temp-
tation for the religious community to be its own worst
enemy and to go into denial, marginalizing itself yet further
from the world and insulating itself from the awkward
questions. The writer Walter Brueggemann believes that
the book of Lamentations is one attempt to urge such communities of denial to become what he calls 'communities of
honest sadness', facing up to the reality that things have
changed for ever.[2]

But what if, when we come to this crisis crossroads, we
do not take the directions of despair or denial but prefer,

despite everything, to continue in the 'faith' direction? On the one hand we have the example of Habakkuk who rightly understands that 'faith' is a relationship word like 'love' and 'trust' and 'truth'. The opposite of faith thus understood is not *doubt*, but *fear*. Faith understood as the opposite of doubt is an objective thing. It suggests that it is possible to assess the evidence and then decide whether to believe or not. Such faith is constantly under threat from experience. Faith understood as the opposite of fear is a personal quality which is most likely to be put in jeopardy by betrayal. Its defining use is in relation to the covenant technical term which is translated in English as 'steadfast love'. It is the consistent message of the eighth-century BCE prophets and their theological successors that this is how God understands faith. In these terms he has been faithful, but feels betrayed. For Habakkuk, faith means trusting, hanging in and hoping that meaning will emerge sometime – a kind of 'faith seeking understanding'. He says: 'Though the fig tree does not blossom, and no fruit is on the vines; though the produce of the olive fails and the field yields no food: though the flock is cut off from the fold and there is no herd in the stalls, yet I will rejoice in the Lord; I will exult in the God of my salvation' (Habakkuk 3:17f.).

However, this expression of faith can also avoid the 'honest' bit of honest sadness. There has to be a confession that in many respects we had it wrong before, if we are to continue to hold faith with integrity. Faith cannot simply be an interior thing. It must have a public dimension. It must have some forms of expression which make it distinctive and allow us to ask questions about the God who is in the relationship, and the implications for society of having faith in this God. Honest sadness then does not take the line that we understood God fully and he failed to deliver; but rather that we understood God only partially and that the new circumstances give us opportunity to understand him better or more fully. The continuing community of faith responded in just this way and reached new conclusions about the God they thought they had known.

An Ecumenical God

One area in which redefinition was required was that of locality and particularity. Until the Exile, the people of Israel had thought that Yahweh was their God and that he was the best god, but they were prepared to accept that other nations had gods as well, albeit that Yahweh would always beat them in any given contest (for example 1 Kings 18). There was no sense that Yahweh had jurisdiction outside Israel. In 2 Kings 5 we read the account of the healing of the captain of the Syrian guard, Naaman's leprosy at the hands of the prophet Elisha. The Syrian gods had been quite unable to meet this challenge, but Yahweh could. Naaman is so pleased that he vows to worship no god but Yahweh from now on and asks for two mule loads of earth to take home with him (2 Kings 5:17). The implication is that he can only worship the god of Israel on Israelite soil. It's a long way from this kind of understanding to that set out by the exilic portions of the book of Isaiah which present God as a figure who can organize world politics at a stroke. He it is who is summoning Cyrus (a Persian) to overcome the Babylonian empire as a precursor to freeing the people of Israel from their Babylonian captivity. Cyrus is even described as God's anointed (Isaiah 45:1), a scandalous statement akin to describing Saddam Hussein or Osama bin Laden as God's anointed. This requires quite a lot of rethinking about God. It might even have been the main stimulus towards a new theology which had begun to emerge by the end of the Exile – monotheism. *God is not just the best God of many. He is the only God.* We might call this the new stimulus to ecumenism.

Such a discovery about God has serious implications, which we might express in three new theological statements.

If God is the only God then he is the *God of all creation*. The implications of this are worked out primarily in the wisdom literature of the Old Testament, but are also to be seen in the fourth and final strand of the Pentateuch, P. From the middle of the twentieth century it has been commonplace to give creation theology a relatively late place in the development of the religious ideas of Israel. This can come as real surprise to the non-specialist who has got used to opening the Bible at an account of the creation and assuming that that's how faith started. Actually religious faith has a very topsy-turvy way of translating into written form. If we think about the New Testament, people became Christian believers as a result of what happened at the end of Jesus' life, but the Gospels don't start there. The theological ideas conveyed by the birth stories are sometimes thought to be quite late in the New Testament's theological development, and so it is with the Old Testament. Just because it's first in the book doesn't mean it's how people first knew God. The theologian Gerhard von Rad was particularly wedded to the idea that Israel knew the Lord first as redeemer and saviour and only later as creator. He believed that primitive credal statements were to be found in the book of Deuteronomy which pointed to belief in a God who had acted in history and was known through the events of the Exodus primarily as a liberating and covenant-making God. Statements of belief did not begin with a God who had created the world. In the Exile sections of Isaiah, God is presented in dramatic courtroom scenes calling all creation as his witness that he is the only God (for example Isaiah 45:18–21), but the later Wisdom writings develop this theme.

Reflection on Text

Read **Deuteronomy 6:4–25**, and try to imagine what religion actually meant to the people for whom this was their basic creed. How would you describe what is meant by 'salvation' here? How is God known? What would you hope for? Then think, what does believing in a creator God add to this picture? Which do you find the most attractive?

The theological axiom that God is the God of all creation is taken to mean that something of God's design can be discerned in any particular bit of creation. To see how the natural world operates is to see something of God's design and intention. In other words it becomes the basis for a primitive form of science. Wisdom writers, in the book of Proverbs for example, believe they have divine sanction to observe the world and to report its regularities and possible rules, almost as acts of faith. Much of this belongs to the world of what we would now call social science – observing how children might best be brought up or how marriage relationships are best conducted. Pragmatically, which kinds of behaviour lead to success and which to ruin. The underlying implication is that God has designed the world thus, leaving humankind with the fascinating job of working through the clues to a greater appreciation of the designer himself. The important thing to realize as we read these works is that they are not just clever sayings of the kind we might find on the backs of matchboxes or certain kinds of calendar, largely for wry entertainment; but rather they are ways of exploring the world and its ways, made possible by the affirmation that the one God is a creator God, and as such the new search is both liberating and entirely serious.

The opening chapters of the book of Genesis illustrate

the new awareness about God very well. The older of the two so-called accounts of creation, as we have seen, is that found at Genesis 2:4ff. Here the chief interest is focused on the man and the woman. Their relationship to the rest of creation is touched on, but the manner of that creation is left undisclosed. The interest is on how obedient they are and how possible it will be for them to live in God's world on God's terms. The account in Genesis, chapter 1 is the work of the post-exilic P writers. The stress here is on the interrelatedness of the whole of creation. Sin can no longer just be a matter of the personal disobedience of the man and the woman. Sin must now also be understood as the breaking of these interlocking dependencies and relations between different aspects of creation of which human relationship breakdown is just one example. The new preface has set the rest of the story in a new context. The assertion that what God made is good in God's eyes becomes a new assertion of faith, a new assertion to take on trust.

There is a darker side to this theological field. If God has designed the world as it is, then true, it is great fun to find out more about God by finding out more about his creation, but that must also mean that God is in some sense answerable for his creation when it fails to be benign. This is familiar territory. My neighbour's children ask: Why did God make rats? No doubt in other parts of the world children ask: Why did God make mosquitoes? Perhaps their parents wonder why God allows disease at all and why he appears to condone the injustice that prevents proper treatments and that leads to wasteful premature deaths. Following every natural disaster someone asks: How could God allow this earthquake to happen or volcano to erupt or hurricane to wreak havoc? Individuals see the suffering of those they love and ask how such pain could be part of God's plan. These questions, too, are acknowledged and explored by Wisdom writers and we shall consider that response in greater detail in the next chapter. For the moment let us simply observe that it is a theological development to reach the point where the community of faith can begin to have creation theology, alongside a history of the mighty acts of God in one nation's past.

Designer History

The second new theological axiom is that if God is the only God then he must be the *God of all history*. This is an equivalent idea to that of creation, in that they both involve design. The combination of God's being able to intervene in international affairs, and the acceptance of the D position that the Exile was a punishment, led to a new belief that God had designed not only the natural world, but that he had designed history as well. This had the important consequence that all things therefore happen for a purpose. Creation itself has a purpose and a goal. For the first time it became possible for theologians to, as it were, stand outside human history and observe it, and again try to discern its rules and regulations. The most obvious theological genre to result from this new development was the one that came to be called 'apocalyptic'. From the Greek word, 'to reveal', apocalyptic writers claimed to have special insight into God's design for history, and special skill of discernment in terms of relating that plan to present circumstances. It became commonplace to write about the history of the world as divided into neat compartments or ages. The plus side of this thinking was the sense it gave of someone or something being in control. Life was not chaotic, random and capricious. Life had both meaning and purpose. Questions of destiny need not be left to the writers of horoscopes. The downside was that, as with straight creation theology, God is held answerable in a new way for historical disasters. This is a way of thinking that can also lead to a kind of religious anxiety that leaves some people so desperate to know what's going to happen next that they don't have a life in the present at all.

It is perhaps no accident then that apocalyptic writing was at its height during turbulent historical times following the Exile and return. The underlying assumption in these writings is that faith is being contradicted by experience. Assertions that God is in control, that all will be well, and that victories over powers of evil and death are assured, are mocked by experiences of oppression, suffering, occupation and the systematic dismantling of (what by then has come to be known as) Jewish culture. The rationale provided by apocalyptic writers is that the end of an age is near and that a new justice will prevail in the new age when vindication will be delivered. The important thing in the interim is for the community of faith to avoid both immorality and idolatry, both of which will be major temptations, but for which the punishments are dire. This development of the D position – that if bad things happen it's essentially our fault – can only hold the line for so long. There is, as Brueggemann has noted, a moral uneasiness (what he calls incongruity) beginning to develop at the time of the Exile itself. Moreover the assumption with this, as with creation theology, is a) that there is a design and b) that we know what it is. This leaves believers in the position of constantly having to defend God to his detractors, since the likelihood is that faith will constantly be tested by experience. Despite these weaknesses this too is a theological development which can only result from a new and wider understanding of God. The problem of evil is one which both apocalyptic and wisdom writers grapple with. There are few apocalyptic writings in the Old Testament as such, this being a relatively late development. The book of Daniel is the best complete example. But there are fragments in other books, such as Isaiah, chapters 24–27. Some of these begin to map out the vision of a new world order which will redefine the special identity of God's people (for example, Isaiah 25:6–10). Within the Old Testament the fundamental issues are best considered against the background of the book of Job, which we shall look at in the next chapter.

Reflection on Experience

Think for a moment about the phrase in the last paragraph: *This leaves believers in the position of constantly having to defend God to his detractors.* What do you think that means? Have you ever been in that position yourself? How did it feel? Do you think that this is what it means to be a Christian? What would it feel like if you no longer had to explain God in this way?

All People that on Earth Do Dwell

The third axiom to result from the new appreciation of God is the most obviously ecumenical. If there is just one God then he must be the *God of all peoples*. Ironically, this is probably the most difficult for the people of Israel to come to terms with. If God has become a way of understanding our distinctive identity, then to have a new understanding which makes God equally available to all on the same terms seems to suppose that there's nothing special about us after all. The book of Jonah, and perhaps the book of Ruth, are evidence of dealing with this insight. In the book of Jonah, which essentially operates as a kind of 'once upon a time' novel within the Old Testament, the prophet is sent by God to the traditional enemies of Israel with a message for them to repent. Jonah is unwilling even to deliver the message, reflecting the kind of jingoism we find in the book of the prophet Nahum, but eventually does so. The people do in fact repent, and there is the challenge. They can no longer be demonized. God knows them, has opened up lines of communication with them and they have acknowledged him. How then can they be enemies? The book of Jonah ends inconclusively with the issue unresolved and Jonah simply sulking whilst God puts his point of view which we feel instinctively Jonah will reject.

The book of Ruth presents further scandal to national or religious purists. This too is a kind of novel, which has as its punchline the uncomfortable assertion that David, the great hero and icon of the Israelite and then Jewish people has foreign blood in his veins. His great grandmother was from the nation of Moab. More than that, the novel presents her in a very positive light as a striking example of faithfulness and humility. Once again there is no opportunity to demonize or even criticize this person. These writings are radical and challenging, but are only possible as a result of the Exile, which in a sense demands them.

God the Redeemer

There is one further new theological development which is unrelated to monotheism as such but which probably results not so much from the experience of Exile as its aftermath, and that is the concept of a *God who is able to redeem*. Alongside the developing awareness of the problem of evil expressed in terms of: Why do bad things happen to good people? and: Why does there have to be evil in the world at all? is the further question: How do we explain it when good results from evil? The understanding of natural justice which had served Israel's theology thus far was that evil would be punished, and that good *only* results from good. But with the Exile we have a disastrous experience, which leads to new understandings of God and new opportunities to live in the land after the return with a new awareness of lessons learned. Good has come from all this. The idea that good could result from evil intent was, and is, a difficult one to come to terms with. It is also, strangely, a comforting one in some circumstances. A prayer written by a Jew in one of the extermination camps during the Holocaust describes the horrible treatment the prisoners have endured at the hands of their captors and asks God not to forget that. It goes on to ask him to remember also the incredible sense of fellowship which had developed among the prisoners as a result of shared suffering and even speaks of 'the good that has come from all this'. It concludes movingly '. . . and when they [that is, the guards and those responsible for the suffering] come to judgement, let all the good that we have done be their forgiveness'. An example of how the Old Testament theologians dealt with this is to be found in yet another novel – the story of Joseph in Genesis, chapters 37–50.

Reflection on Experience

Can you think of a time when good has resulted from something bad? It's sometimes difficult to admit that but it might be helpful to share if you are doing this as a group exercise. Did anything good come out of September 11, for example? Is it easier to explain and come to terms with, when evil generates more evil (lots of possible examples here and you might like to think of a few)? How have you responded, what has it meant to you when good has resulted from evil? What do you think it means to say that something or someone is 'beyond redemption?' Is this comforting or frightening?

This story, interestingly, displaces Joseph. As a result of his brothers' evil intent he is taken as a prisoner to a foreign land, in this case Egypt. There he narrowly escapes death whilst maintaining his honour and distinctive identity. He has special insight into God's plans within human history (which are now understood to involve Egypt as well as Israel) and as a result he gains high office. There is a kind of punishment for his brothers as Joseph plays a game with them (which actually sounds far from convincing), but the key lies not in that but rather in the rationale which the author provides for the story. God had been behind the whole thing all along. Whilst the brothers had meant to do harm, God was working to achieve good. He was able to convert evil intent to good outcome. He could redeem. Joseph says to his brothers: 'do not be distressed or angry with yourselves, because you sold me here; for God sent me before you to preserve life' (Genesis 45:5). And indeed it appears this is part of an even bigger plan which will locate the family of Israel outside their land and so in time enable them to affirm the faithfulness of God by repossessing it according to his promise.

The book of Esther, yet another novel, this time set after the Exile and consequent dispersion, and again outside Israel, highlighting the fragility of the Jews' position, makes a similar point. God is not mentioned in this book but is the unseen and understood presence who is working to convert the evil intentions of Haman against the Jews. In the end Haman is hoisted by his own petard and hung on the gallows he had intended for Mordecai the Jew. Despite some national triumphalism, the author makes the final point that, as a result of what happened, Mordecai is able to look after the welfare of his people. Good has resulted from evil intent.

Responding and Coping

These theological responses to the Exile, although expressed as separate axioms, have common strands. They all stand in a tradition which refused to believe that the Exile spelled the end of religion, even though according to the rules of the old religion it ought to have done. They all display a degree of excitement at the new possibilities which were opened up for theological understanding: that is, they are theologically creative and vibrant. They all accept that the new situation poses problems for God, and that it is no longer possible for talk about God to continue without qualification and amendment. They accept that the solutions they propose and the developments they suggest also raise new questions and new problems for God. These problems are about power and the problems associated with evil and suffering. Having newly realized that God has the ability to intervene in human history and destiny, the questions arise: Why does he not do so for good, and why does evil so often seem to prevail? They also all provide new challenges for the community of faith who have to learn afresh what religion is about, and redefine terms like 'faith' and 'election'. But are these any more than interesting theological footnotes from the dawn of history? Does what we have discovered about the Exile experience, and about the responses to it from the Old Testament have any coherence, and more importantly, does that have resonance with our experience today? Is reading the Old Testament in this way potentially transforming or does it maintain the remoteness of which we earlier complained?

There is an increasing, though still relatively short, list of mostly American scholars who believe that the Exile provides the most promising possibility for the application of Old Testament texts to contemporary experience. They can be distinguished from those scholars who dispute the historical facts of the Exile or who dispute the severity of its treatment of Jews in Babylon, or who agree with older scholars such as C. C. Torrey that the whole thing has been overplayed. He in fact thought that it was 'a small and relatively insignificant affair'.[3] Daniel Smith-Christopher is the latest to take a different view, and to suggest that an 'exilic theology promises to be the most provocative, creative and helpful set of ideas that modern Christians can derive from the ancient Hebrews' religious reflections on their experience'.[4] Smith-Christopher's work offers a compelling defence of the actual enormity of the experience of the Exile, and he draws on contemporary literature from disaster studies, refugee studies and the study of post-traumatic stress disorder to illustrate the integrity and authenticity of the experience of response described particularly in the books of Ezekiel (written during exile in Babylon) and Lamentations (written in response to the sacking of Jerusalem in 587, in Palestine). He recognizes in the texts resonances with contemporary experience. He notes, for example, some of the coping strategies employed by those who have experienced disaster.

One coping strategy is connected with the desire to see the suffering as having achieved something. Anyone who has watched the televised responses of those in Ireland and elsewhere who have suffered terrorist atrocities and perhaps seen their children killed, will be familiar with the sentiment that 'if this helps to bring people to their senses and so bring peace a little nearer, then this death will not have been in vain'. Children's tragic deaths often prompt parents to start funds and charities for research into disease or to support parents whose children are very ill. At heart this is what we have discerned in the Old Testament in its determination that these dreadful events should have meaning. The thing that would be intolerable is for there to be no meaning, no purpose and that the death or the suffering was utterly futile and insignificant. The search for meaning and the determination to assert significance is a connecting factor between the Exile and many modern forms of suffering. Another group of coping strategies is connected with telling the story of the past, in an attempt to set out who we were and *that* we were. Also to have a resource for reflection on what might have caused the tragedy – often leading to subjective blame. 'If only I'd done such and such . . .' is a common sentiment expressed at a time of bereavement. The sense of meaning is maintained by relating it to some supposed pattern of regularity, some rule of nature which has been transgressed, rather than by questioning the rule. These are responses which can be discerned in the histories of the D school.

Smith-Christopher's work alerts us to what we might call a problem of methodology in attempting to relate Old Testament Exile to modern experience. How are we to define what it is we hope to apply to the modern situation? Smith-Christopher uses the term 'exilic theology' to convey what he sees as essential. For other writers it is the state of being in some kind of exile, some kind of juxtaposition with the society in which one is set, that is the key thing to apply to the modern situation. What I want to draw attention to could perhaps best be described as a process rather than a theology or a state. It is a way of doing theology, a way of understanding what theology is, and I want to claim that religious communities that understand and do theology in this way have particular characteristics. What interests me is how religious people react to the kinds of experience that seem to point to their abandonment by God, and that raise the kind of new questions that suggest we have completely to rethink God. I believe that this is not just something that happens to nations. Human life is full of such times, and even when things big enough to be recorded in history, like perhaps September 11 do happen, they are actually experienced at an individual and human level by those who have suffered. They are not just events to be coped with by society or within the political arena. They

require a pastoral response. I believe that the pastoral application of the Old Testament to our situation derives from
understanding the kind of process which I want to call
'exilic'; which means understanding both the kinds of
reflection that result from these traumatic experiences, and
the religious communities which result. Moreover I believe
it to be a process which we can see continuing through the
New Testament and recognize in our own experience.
These are actually more than 'coping strategies'. They are
the best examples we have of how, and indeed why, theology is done, in the Old Testament.

If we accept the story of the Old Testament as set out so
far, and believe it to be essentially a series of reflections
connected by the experience of Exile, we see in those theological reflections a new series of categories emerging.
There is a new ecumenism, and new exploration around the
themes of the God of all creation, the God of all history, the
God of all peoples, and the God who can redeem. These
reflections suggest that:

- The events are *significant*. They matter so fundamentally
  that understandings of God are at stake.
- The events are *serious*. These are not superficial but are
  part of the destiny of a people, and the world.
- The events are *decisive*. They force us to make decisions
  about faith.
- The events are *theologically subversive,* undermining
  what we thought we knew about God and religion.
- The events have *creative possibility*. There is an alternative to despair, apathy or atheism.
- The events connect history and faith in a new way that
  will not allow retreat into secular atheism or religious
  piety.

Moreover there is a *style* which accompanies this reflection.
On the one hand it is creative, exploratory and almost

mischievously innovative. But on the other it is tentative, humble, accepting the provisionality and unresolvedness of the issues with which it deals. At the end of the book of Jonah we have an unsatisfactory stand-off. The new P account of creation in Genesis, chapter 1 replaces the confident and dominant man, the first and most important part of creation, who had such dominion that he could even name the animals (Genesis 2:20); with an alternative in which man and woman come last on the scene, tentatively entering, almost as guests, a world that is already formed and about which they have to learn. The other P additions to those early chapters of Genesis, and their editorial arrangement, have the effect of replacing certainties with possibilities, alternatives and questions. New literary 'novel' forms are employed to help define questions more precisely, the story form itself suggesting ambiguity rather than definite fixed and final answers.

As we have seen, there is a modern trend to get under the skin of this experience thus understood. On the one hand there are plenty who see this as a time of perceived crisis for faith. In that situation it is important to share the excitement of a community whose reaction to its crisis proved so creative. On the other hand there are those who today are troubled by the move to a so-called postmodern society, away from a time when religion was seen to declare the one demonstrable truth which governed all life, and when it was the church's job to persuade people of that. To understand the church's mission in a postmodern culture it will be crucial to understand a community of faith which has a different starting point. So we might attempt to share the sense of provisionality, and the lack of confidence in schemes and grand plans supposing immutable rules by which human life and destiny are governed, to which the writings from the exilic experience give us access.

It may be that those who have experienced an September 11, or whose identity is shaped by memories of displacement or folk memories of slavery, have the best access to the psychology of exile and its theological process. It may also be true that elements of the process are accessible to those of us with a more comfortable history, but who nevertheless experience disorientating tragedy at points in our lives. If we want to understand this exilic process more fully, what better place to start than with one of those novels in the Old Testament which in its own day represented the cutting edge of religious expression, as it sought to relate the process of exile to ordinary life.

3

Job – the New (Religious) Man

Introduction

Job was one of the first biblical characters I was ever aware of. This was because in our house we had an antique mug, some family heirloom, in the shape of a man's face covered in colourful boils and sores. It made you itch just to look at it. It was, I was told, a Job mug. Goodness knows why people produced this sort of thing, and yet I have to admit it had a kind of attractiveness despite its ugliness. You could say something similar about the book of Job. In some respects it's a coarse and brutal book, and yet there is something magnificent about it. It's certainly avant-garde. I know there's some discussion among scholars about where the book came from and what kind of people or sources might have contributed to its production, but since none of these questions has any bearing on my interpretation of the text I shall ignore them. I think of this as a mould-breaking work, the *Look Back in Anger* of its day. I imagine it having its debut on some trendy arts programme called something like 'Babylon 4'.

What's It All About?

One of the disputed issues in Job interpretation (and I suppose you'd say it was pretty fundamental) is what the book is actually about. There is widespread agreement that it is in fact a work of fiction (it more or less begins with the words: 'Once upon a time in a land far away'), and that it sets out to explore certain questions, but there are differences amongst commentators as to what those questions are. The story the book tells is of a man called Job who is 'blameless and upright'. He has enjoyed all the fruits that a blameless life provides, according to the theory of natural justice that the good always prosper and the bad don't. He is living proof of the observation of the Psalmist that the righteous are never poor and never forsaken (Psalm 37:25–33). He has land, cattle, family. He was 'the greatest of all the people of the east' (Job 1:3). He was intensely pious, even going through the appropriate rituals for sins that might have been committed by other members of the family. They were in all respects a model religious family of the old religious understanding. The scene then moves to heaven and gives us a glimpse of God making a deal with Satan. Satan believes that Job is only good and pious because it profits him. 'Does Job fear God for nothing?' he asks, clearly believing the answer to be no (Job 1:9). God is proud of Job, almost presented as a kind of star pupil, and is ready to leave him open to testing as long as he is not made to suffer physically. Satan then sets about stripping Job of all his benefits. He loses his possessions, his cattle and his children in a series of sudden disasters. But God is proved right. Job remains faithful. For a second time we are transported to heaven. For a second time Satan mocks God's trust in Job as a model of faith. He says, in effect: 'So far he hasn't been harmed himself. If he started to suffer you'd soon see him change his tune.' So God gives permission. Satan does his worst and Job is smitten with a dreadful plague of sores. Still he refuses to curse God, despite even his wife's entreaties.

Thus set up, the narrative ends. We hear no more reference to Satan, and even at the end of the book there is no mention of the original wager or its outcome. These first two chapters are a device to introduce the issue. But what is the issue? Some believe that the issue is the one stated: in other words, is there such a thing as disinterested piety? Eaton, for example, wants to develop this into the question: Is there such a thing as disinterested love, or does the notion of interest always intervene in human affairs? Whybray thinks the issue has more to do with the nature of God. Are human concepts of justice the same as God's? What is the human capacity to understand God? Many others, of whom van Wolde is a recent example, think the issue is the problem of suffering. How are we to understand God when evil hits good people? Why do good people suffer? Although each of these possibilities offers partial explanation of the writer's purpose none gives an answer that is comprehensively satisfying. Such an answer is only given, I think, by understanding Job as the most sophisticated response that the Old Testament can offer to the theological developments we have noted as a consequence of Exile. From this perspective Job is an answer to the question: How is it possible to be faithful or pious in these new times? What does the new religious man look like?

Job and His Friends

The vehicle for these discussions is a series of speeches made in sequence, involving mainly Job and three other speakers or 'friends'. Whereas the opening chapters are wholly artificial, setting up the situation like some malign producers of a reality TV show which could perhaps be called: 'I'm a righteous man. Get me out of here!' the discussions with the friends are more recognizable, though only just falling short of being predictable caricatures. In differing ways they represent old religion, and ways of being religious that are no longer appropriate. They have been discredited by experience and by the further theological reflection on that experience which we have noted.

There are two kinds of irony that are immediately apparent. The first is that the three friends are quite happy to live in this inappropriate way, and defend religion soundly on the basis of it. The second is that the crude and indefensible pictures of God which the first two chapters present are the only ones available under the old system to a good person who suffers. That is perhaps one of the reasons why they are not reintroduced at the end of the book. By then a new understanding of what it is to be religious has emerged in which such caricatures have no place.

So what has provided the crisis for old religion? Initially (we know) it is the Exile with its new theological affirmations that God is the God of all creation, the God of all history and the God of all peoples; that he is the one God and that he can redeem. As described in Chapter 2 these affirmations lead to questions about the power and intention of God seen as a benign designer of both history and creation. Experience has shot to pieces any view of the world based on assumptions that it is fair or just. What is true of nations in the case of the Exile is also true of individuals, and one of the contributions of the book of Job is to introduce the new theology into the context of individual faith meeting with individual tragedy, outlining in the process some of the new pastoral considerations that need to be addressed. The world is actually experienced by people as unfair and as if at the hand of a careless and irresponsible God, and that is why the opening of the story takes the form it does. There is something very serious and 'real' about this, which the jaunty, almost playful tone of the text makes even more scandalous.

Comparison could be made with the story of Cain and Abel in Genesis, chapter 4. Both Cain and Abel make offerings to God. 'And the Lord had regard for Abel and his offering, but for Cain and his offering he had no regard' (Genesis 4:4f.). Attempts by an older generation of Genesis scholars to find some reason for this are quite futile. The point is, there is no reason. That is how life is. Two people pray for recovery and only one gets better.

Reflection on Experience

Has something like this ever happened to you? Have you ever had occasion to question the *fairness* of God? What kind of occasion was that? Could you have described it as a crisis for faith? How did you deal with it? Some typical reactions might include:

- It wasn't really unfair. It's just that I didn't have the whole picture. Only God had that.
- God must know what he's doing.
- It's all part of God's plan and not for me to question.

As you read more of Job see if you can recognize these responses, and if Job's own response gives you any new way to look on your own experience.

The story in Genesis 4 is about how to react to that reality rather than to find some rule of creation which governs occasions like that; such as Cain having done something wrong, withheld something, had the wrong attitude or whatever. And that is what we see in Job. The friends represent a view that finds meaning and assurance in what in today's jargon would be called a *metanarrative*. That is, they believe there is a plan to creation and history, and the role of religion is to affirm the rules of the design and safe-guard them. The keeping of the rules and the observance of religious ritual will guarantee that the world remains both safe and fair. Even before beginning to read we might dismiss such a view as ludicrous. We might protest that faith understood in those terms would be a delusion to insulate us from reality and inevitably marginalize religion to a ghetto where obsessively careful and paranoid people could live boring lives. Unfortunately, our experience informs us that that is precisely how many people understand and experience the Christian religion today.

Archdeacon Eliphaz

The speeches begin with Job himself cursing the day of his birth in forthright and robust terms (chapter 3). This is all too much for the first friend, Eliphaz. All three friends have in common a belief that Job must have sinned, or broken the rules in some way. As readers, we are party to the secret that this is not so. In real life many pastors are not so sure, and Eliphaz reminds us of them. As he is the first to speak, we may assume he is the eldest. He speaks from experience (ironically enough). I like to think of him as an archdeacon. He points out that Job himself was once on-side. He instructed others. Now he must believe what he told them. The view Eliphaz holds, in which he wants Job to admit complicity, is that only the guilty suffer.

His 'pastoral approach' has three strands. The first is the appeal to *his* experience which he takes to be universal. 'Think now, who that was innocent ever perished? Or where were the upright cut off? As I have seen, those who plough iniquity and sow trouble reap the same' (Job 4:7f.). Then secondly, he claims the authority of a self-authenticating vision. Finally he offers pious, politically correct sentiment in which is wrapped up the contentious point: 'do not despise the discipline of the almighty' (Job 5:17). The assumption is that Job is experiencing punishment and should take it humbly as evidence that he has sinned. The old Job, the Job who made careful sacrifices just in case his children had sinned inadvertently, might well have been persuaded. The new Job is not prepared to play the game. His suffering and his self-awareness have moved him beyond the point where that is possible. In the process we see the aridity of what is pastorally on offer from Eliphaz. All he presents is a series of closed opinions which cannot be contested. Who can say that he didn't have a vision, or that his experience has not been so blinkered? What we can say is that it has been different for us. The crisis for old religion begins to be clear. It has the words and the ritual but it isn't listening and it is completely wedded to 'explanation' forms of religion, which in turn are part of a mechanical system of making the world safe. After all, if Job were to go through the form of words Eliphaz wants to hear, then despite the dishonesty of it all, Eliphaz would be happy. His job would have been done. You could almost imagine him saying to his archdeacon friends: 'I had a result with Job!'

Reflection on Text

To get a flavour of Eliphaz's contribution you could read **Job 4:7–21**, **5:17–27**. Try to put yourself in Eliphaz's shoes and see the problem as he sees it. Do you recognize this kind of approach? Do you have any sympathy with it? Can you think of any circumstances in which it might be helpful, or is it just a dreadful warning to all would-be pastors?

Job's actual response is to give further robust evidence of what most people really think about life and its difficulties, suggesting that Eliphaz is someone who is either oblivious to them through some social privilege, or that he chooses to ignore them. Or even perhaps, that he lives in a religious alternative world which refuses to acknowledge their significance. Job 7:1–6 is patently the experience that readers will identify with. In Job's mouth, the way the story is told, such declaration of reality is presented as blasphemy.

Straightforward Bildad

The second friend, Bildad, understands nothing of this. He probably sees himself as a pretty straightforward sort of chap when it comes to religion. He dismisses what Job has to say as a lot of wind (Job 8:2). His basic position is the same as that of Eliphaz but his pastoral approach is different. He appeals to tradition. 'For inquire now of bygone generations, and consider what their ancestors have found; for we are but of yesterday and we know nothing' (Job 8:8). These words are heavy with irony. At stake here is a view of religion in which tradition counts more than either faith or experience, and in which revelation and consequent understanding are all things of the past. Everything that there is to know about religion is already known and thought. It just has to be learned and taken to heart. This view too is wrapped up in pious words, including what might be regarded by the speaker as a note of hope, but it will not do for Job. Job represents the new religion in which God is revealing himself in a new way, leading to new understandings. The traditions will not bear the weight current experience is placing upon them, and Bildad doesn't realize that.

In particular, Job articulates the fears for individual piety that belief in a God of all creation might imply. He wants to believe that God knows him and created him for a purpose and takes a continuing interest in him. 'You have granted me life and steadfast love [technical reference to the Covenant here], and your care has preserved my spirit. Yet these things you hid in your heart: I know that this was your purpose' (Job 10:12f.). But his fear is that God has become too distant and terrible. He is interested only in punishment, and as a result of his greatness there is none to intercede with him: 'there is no umpire between us, who might lay his hand on us both' (Job 9:33). Indeed this is one of the great crises of post-exilic faith. God becomes more and more remote.

In the earliest (J) traditions of the Pentateuch, God is a very close figure. He can stop and chat with Adam in the Garden of Eden (Genesis 3:8) almost man to man. The later (E) traditions make God a little more distant. In these traditions (for example Genesis 28:12ff.) God's purposes are accessed through dreams, though there is still a real awareness of God's presence in the ordinary and everyday (Genesis 28:16). However, post-exilic theology often sees God as a very distant figure indeed. As the opening chapters of Job display, God is a remote bureaucrat, the chairperson of a heavenly council, with an array of intermediaries between him and humankind. We might think of them as a prime minister and cabinet in which particular ministers have responsibility for particular areas. So Michael would be the defence minister, Raphael the minister for health and Gabriel the communication supremo. Satan would be the minister without portfolio, free to wander as he might (the original derivation of his name). The huge 'civil service' that they generate makes direct access to God very difficult and access itself becomes an issue. Expressed at its simplest, Job's fear is that God's greatness has meant that he has lost interest in individual destinies. But Bildad understands nothing of this. For him, God's greatness is guarantee of the system. Moreover, in the access question, we get the impression that he and his friends might just like to be gatekeepers.

Reflection on Text

To get a sense of Bildad's approach read **Job, chapter 8**. Go through the same process as for

Eliphaz above. Do you agree with his understanding of tradition, or do you prefer Job's appeal to current experience?

Enter the Expert

Zophar is the third 'friend' to speak. Probably the youngest, Zophar no doubt regards himself as a modern theologian, who has really kept up with trends, and understands all the jargon. His pastoral approach is based on the new theological idea of wisdom. He articulates the premises on which, for example, the book of Proverbs is based: that the way to be religious is to pursue wisdom and to eschew stupidity. Proverbs gives sufficient examples of how this works out in practice for us to be able to piece together the ethical world-view that this involves. Hard work and filial loyalty are to be encouraged, for example. Women, on the other hand, are snares, best avoided, apart from those women who will be 'good' (that is, completely subservient) wives. Perhaps the most comprehensive picture of this wisdom world-view is found in Job, chapter 31, as he concludes his defence. He has actually answered all the demands of the wisdom writers, but still knows there is more. He is not content to reduce religion to a set of moral rules, an ethical system. He maintains a belief in a living God (Job 19:25–27). Ironically he holds a much 'higher' doctrine of God than do his detractors but they do not recognize that. In answer to Zophar Job mocks those 'who bring their god in their hands' (Job 12:6). His basic complaint against the religion represented by the friends is that it claims to understand God fully. It has in fact made an idol of God by claiming to be able to identify the systems by which he works. God's Old Testament name, Yahweh, declares: 'I am what I am and I shall be what I shall be.' A God who can be completely known is not God at all.

There is also a hint in Zophar's speech of another underlying assumption in his pastoral approach, that Zophar is the expert. He is able to use the technical terms of the new wisdom theology confidently, and to close religious arguments simply by claiming that his opponents do not understand fully enough. This certainly seems to be the way Job understands him, for his retort and put-down is immediate: 'No doubt you are the people, and wisdom will die with you. But I have understanding as well as you; I am not inferior to you. Who does not know such things as these' (Job 12:2f.). Job may long for an umpire but he doesn't need the kind of exclusive expert for whom knowledge is little more than opportunity to exercise power in pastoral relationships. These are the spokespeople for the old understanding of religion who Job dismisses as 'worthless physicians' (Job 13:4) and 'miserable comforters' (Job 16:2). The importance of their contributions is twofold. On the one hand they articulate a particular understanding of dogmatic theology. But perhaps, more importantly, because the story is set in a pastoral context, they show what that dogmatic theology amounts to in practice and what it has to offer to those who are trying to come to terms with their experience of life. In other words it offers an insight into not only a dogmatic theology which is bankrupt, but also an insight into the practical theology which results from it, in terms of pastoral care, ministry and even ritual.

Reflection on Text

Zophar's first contribution is to be found in **Job, chapter 11**. Again, try to put yourself in his shoes, if possible imagining some modern counterpart. You might even try to put his argument into modern speech. If you do this as a group exercise, different members of the group could each take the part of the different friends. Would you like any of these people to be a pastor to you in need? Have you experienced the ministrations of anyone like them? What does this say to you about what the church might need to do?

Ministry in Job

We see dogmatic theology at its most dogmatic and unyielding. Creation theology has only been partially accepted, resulting in the lack of rational integrity that Job exposes. We see a new and potentially reductionist wisdom theology which regards religion as essentially keeping a set of rules. In effect this is just a new way of describing the old position – that the world is governed by rules and systems, the keeping of which will guarantee safety and continuity. We see pastors (perhaps it would not be too much to say 'ministers'), who are more interested in power and influence than in Job himself. They see their task in terms of knowing the rules of the system and applying them. This system is so big on punishment and moral censure, based as it is on the awareness of the constant possibility of transgression, that it confuses awe with fear. We see a religious outlook which we could almost say is designed to fail in any missionary sense, in that it makes a virtue out of pitting faith against experience, meaning that a religious person has constantly to be denying the validity of their experience, something Job is not prepared to do. We suspect that the piety expressed by the friends is a form of self-deception. Allied to their belief that tradition is closed, we further suspect that they fear losing control. From the speeches, we see what Job wants from all this. He wants assurance that God has a personal relationship with him, and that God is not just some remote control freak, which would be really frightening, and which is how, did they but know it, the friends essentially represent him. Job wants a faith that does not always contradict experience but which is confirmed by experience. He wants a faith that has rational integrity, and ministry that is prepared to engage in real debate about that. That is not to say that he wants a faith in which there is no place left for God to be God. But at least he wants to have faith in God as trustworthy. Importantly, all this is presented as the agenda of someone who is already part of the religious enterprise. Job is not a sceptical outsider. He is from the first identified as someone who refuses to curse God.

So how does the book of Job resolve the issues it raises? The main arguments of the friends are introduced in their first round of speeches, and though they all contribute again, little is added that we do not already know. These speeches end at chapter 31 after which we get a brief burst of ironic narrative which tells us that the friends gave up because Job was righteous in his own eyes. Expressed like that it invites sympathy for the friends and judgement on Job. We then have two more lots of speeches. The first is from a new character called Elihu who represents angry young men, and reminds us, the readers, of what is at stake here. Then God speaks, from a whirlwind. He describes his creation in his own words. For the first time Job is reassured of the integrity of creation. For the first time, he hears and sees God. We are left with the conviction that the whirlwind from which God speaks was precisely the struggle which the previous chapters outline. Whereas the friends try to find a system to explain Job's suffering, he himself finds an authentic vision and audition of God from the midst of both his suffering and his anguished questioning.

There is a short narrative conclusion which is largely unrelated to the introduction. Some scholars find this disappointing since it describes the restoration of Job's fortunes in an 'all's well that ends well' kind of way. This is as misplaced a disappointment as it would be to say that the resurrection is rather disappointing after the crucifixion. These should not be understood in a narrow mechanical sequential way. The restoration is a literary device to ratify the final position which the text outlines about religion. The main struggle appears not to have been between Satan and God so much as between Job's view of God and that of his friends. And in that struggle, Job is pronounced the winner. This indeed is the final irony of the book. Throughout the work, the author has tried to persuade us that Job is the blasphemer and that his friends are righteous. The conclusion turns this on its head. We see that it is the friends who are self-righteous, and Job who has been true to God, and who is vindicated. However, two things have to happen before vindication and restoration can take effect. The first is that Job has to abandon his self-absorption, which has been a feature of all his speeches, and fully acknowledge the majesty, wisdom and mystery of God. The second is that Job has to minister to his friends. In the narrative God is angry with the three of them. He demands that they make sacrifices in Job's presence and that Job then make intercession for them which God will hear. Only as a result of this loss of self-absorption, and this ministry of reconciliation with his friends is Job's own healing and restoration possible.

Conclusions

This narrative may seem a long way from Jeremiah's accounts of the last days of Jerusalem and the long trek to Babylon, and in a sense it is. But it does represent the Old Testament's considered response to the most important questions that theological reflection on those events of Exile has raised. Jeremiah himself undergoes personal suffering, but it is only in the more artificial and stylized genre of the book of Job that the full range of issues raised by his and others' suffering can be debated systematically, and the implications of the new theology assessed. On the face of it this is subversive literature. Van Selms believes that 'it is nothing short of a miracle that this book was taken up into the Canon of scripture'.[5] But then there is a sense in which new theology should always appear subversive and that is part of the point of the story. The fundamental assertions are extremely orthodox, namely, that even in these new times, belief in God is possible.

The book represents something of a triumph for un-resolvedness over against resolution; for possibility over against definition; for process over against system. In its apparent assertion that God can be met in suffering it does not offer a definitive answer to the problem of suffering, which continues to be a live issue in the later writings of the Old Testament, an issue raised essentially by experience of Exile. What is clear is that answers to the problem based on ritual systems of cleansing, scapegoats, sacrifices and the punishment of sinners will not do. At least two other pos-sibilities will be considered before the ministry of Jesus introduces a new dimension to the discussion. One is that the system of natural justice does in fact operate but after death rather than in this life. This is the preferred option of the apocalyptic literature which has to find an urgent answer from within its context of oppression and suffering. The other more philosophical idea, a development of the notion that God can redeem, finds expression in the servant songs from the exilic portions of the book of Isaiah. This solution is that suffering can be redemptive. It can be part of God's purpose in order to achieve a greater good. The suffering of the obedient servant has ransomed many: 'He was wounded for our transgressions, crushed for our iniquities; upon him was the punishment that made us whole, and by his bruises we are healed' (Isaiah 53:5). Alongside these, Job's response that God can be met in suf-fering, is part of the inheritance that later theologians will conjure with. But this must be recognized as an important contribution of the book, and one that begins to make religion credible to suffering people.

Reflection on Text

There are four of these so-called servant songs in the central portion of Isaiah, the portion normally accepted as having been written during the Exile, that is chapters 40–55. Probably the best known is **Isaiah 52:13 – 53:12**. Read through the passage. Why do you think it is often read on Good Friday? What links are we being encouraged to make as a result of reading it on that occasion?

Allied with this is the inkling of a new understanding of forgiveness. Prior to the Exile such mention as the Old Testament makes of forgiveness is limited to the ritual system. The idea of a forgiveness between close friends who have been fundamentally at odds is much nearer to what will be a developing theme throughout the rest of the Bible, namely a forgiveness based on grace. When Job's friends bring their sacrifices at the end of the book, it is not those sacrifices which will be effective but rather Job's prayer and his willingness to pray it. In the process of praying it he himself is healed. This has strains of 'forgive us our trespasses as we forgive those who trespass against us' but is in any case a new departure both for understanding of pastoral ministry and of ritual associated with it. The Exile itself had forced some new thinking on forgiveness. The insistence of the D writers that the whole thing 'was our fault' and that we are being punished can only last for so long. Towards the end of the Exile other voices are heard announcing an end to punishment and giving new ground for hope: 'Speak tenderly to Jerusalem, and cry to her that she has served her term, that her penalty is paid, that she has received from the Lord's hand double for all her sins' (Isaiah 40:2). This is Israel's first communal experience of forgiveness. Those who speak of it do not regard it as Israel's right, or something the nation in Exile has deserved – in fact they've had twice what they deserve. Even this punishment is unfair. The decision to end the Exile is God's alone. This is forgiveness understood as an act of grace, and is a new theological element to emerge from Exile.

As the story is told we can pick up other nuances which might be helpful as we consider questions about the appropriate shape of church life in our own time.

Reflection on Experience

Consider the last sentence. From your own experience of church, and from your entering the world of the book of Job, what do you think are the points we need to note as we try to apply the exilic process to our own situation?

The book affirms that robust debate with God and forthright anger directed towards God are both legitimate forms of religious discourse. The question as to what role ministry has in enabling, refereeing or interpreting this discourse might also be one we note. From the pastoral perspective, the book highlights especially the importance of paying attention to all aspects of need and not approaching profound human problems with ready-made, off-the-peg answers. People have to be heard where they are and as they are, and in the terms they choose. Refusal to allow this is as often as not tied up with the fears of the pastor at losing control, rather than with attempts to help minister effectively. The immutability of God, this God who is creator and designer of the world, its history and its peoples and who can choose to redeem, is finally seen as a theological axiom which can inspire and guarantee: which can lead to awe and not just fear. As creator, God is not only interested in punishment. As one who holds destinies in his hands he is interested in the fulfilling of destinies and the realizing of creative possibility.

Such mature responses to Exile, and the theological reflections it produced, bring religion back from the brink and encourage its survival against the odds. Life does have meaning. Faith is not stupid. Belief in God is still credible. Forgiveness is possible. This is what I regard as the 'exilic process' of theology. Applications of it to our own situation direct me therefore not so much towards situations where people are living as foreigners in lands other than their homeland; but rather towards those situations where the church is called upon to make pastoral responses urgently in the face of new questions. Exile breeds New Job. New Job requires New Church. It is precisely that kind of crisis and process which gives us what we have come to term, the New Testament.

4

So What's New?

Introduction

Before we start talking about the crisis in relation to the
New Testament we need to understand just why it was a
crisis, and what kind of crisis it was. As we have seen the
Old Testament react to it, the Exile provided enormous
potential for crisis and chaos. It represented a huge threat
to the people of Israel, quite apart from the human
tragedies of displacement and suffering. It provided crisis in
terms of identity, meaning and purpose. A people whose
very identity depended on their having a land and characteristic civilization now had no land. A people whose
landmarks of meaning were mapped in terms of a Covenant
with a caring and loving God now experienced abandonment. Hence this was potentially also a crisis for God
and religion. What was the point? The evidence of the Old
Testament is that the crisis was averted, but at the cost of
dumping much of what had been understood as the very
stuff of religion in the old dispensation – a dumping which
was painful in itself and too risky for some who preferred
to continue to believe and act as if nothing had happened.
The creative outpourings which came as a consequence of
the Exile show us how the crisis was averted by those who
wanted to maintain dynamic and vital faith. We see how
the community moved forward with a new sense of
identity, new landmarks of meaning, a new awareness of

forgiveness and hence a new vision and hope. Incredibly, a small, insignificant nation could begin to dream about a new world order.

Moving on

The *necessity to rescue a sense of identity* (a common reaction, as we have seen, to displacement crises) resulted in two new tellings of the stories of the people. The first, from the Deuteronomists (D), makes sense of the tragedy in terms of blame (another common reaction). OK it's broken, but that's not because it was designed wrongly, it's just that we didn't use it properly. The other story from the Priestly school (P), or the Chronicler's history, re-establishes the fundamentals of 'who we are', based on what has proved both possible and helpful in Exile. Hence the way is opened for a new sense of community based not exclusively on possession of a land, though that continues to be important, but rather on shared marks such as male circumcision, shared religious institutions such as those provided by temple and Sabbath, and the allegiance to a shared dogma which would shortly lead to the beginnings of the establishment of a canon of sacred scripture.

The *crisis for meaning*, which is another way of describing the crisis for God in these new times, was not so easily overcome, but we do see the process at least begin in the Old Testament. Great creative theological activity meant that new theological ideas could be conjured with. These had to take account of restoration as well as suffering and Exile in a way which provided some continuity with the religious institutions and aspirations of the past. In other words, the solution was not to start again as if previous history did not matter. It was, rather, to interpret the past in the light of present understanding and in the process to give new definition to religious terminology and practice. We see this reworking especially in the forming of the

Pentateuch. According to one commentator, a possible rather touching example is the inclusion by the P writers of a number of genealogies. According to Brueggemann this is a direct scriptural response to the experience of being orphaned. The lists of names declare that we are part of a family that has roots and that has stories.[6]

Reflection on Experience

The novel, and subsequent TV dramatization of *Roots* by Alex Haley highlighted the importance of being able to make the kinds of connection that tell us who we are. It told the story of a modern American who traced his roots to the small village of Juffure on the Gambia River in West Africa, from where his ancestor Kunte Kinte had been taken as a slave. If you saw the film or read the book you might share perceptions of it and recall the effect it had on you. How important are roots to you? What are the things that tell you who you are? What part does religion play in this, if any? What would happen if you were to lose connection with these roots? Does reflecting in this way help you to understand the needs of the exilic community better?

Fundamental Change

The experience of Exile itself and the monotheism that resulted from it brought a new interest in God and creation. This in turn led to an interest in God as designer of history; and as the nation's fortunes did not mend, and successive foreign occupiers scandalized or oppressed the Jews in various ways, this interest in God's design for history tended towards questions about suffering and justice. Experience was now more regularly at odds with faith, and faith came to be expressed theologically more regularly in terms of aspiration. That is, the main theological question for the people of Israel was now not so much who they are or what they believe God has made them, as it is what they hope for. In other words we see *the rise of eschatology*, a way of speaking theologically which imagines a future that has significant discontinuities with the present. People of faith now see such a gap between life as it is and life as they believe God intended and designed it, that it is inconceivable that the simple process of historical development can bring about the necessary change. Some new fundamental cataclysmic action is needed, and only God can provide it. This kind of theology has implications both for how people understand God and how they understand their own place in history. It is notable that the Old Testament can now articulate a theology which takes account of fundamental discontinuity. Arguably it was the Exile that made this possible as well as making it necessary.

Donald Gowan sees three connected strands associated with the new hopes, all of which derive from his studies in Ezekiel 36:22–38:23. He believes that eschatological thinking derives from an experience of the world which emphasizes its 'radical wrongness'.[7] God the creator made everything good but it is now hopelessly corrupted. Only radical transformation will bring an end to evil. This transformation needs to be of three kinds. We have seen how, at the theological level, restoration and return have led to *new interest in forgiveness*. This is now developed. God must transform the human person to give a new heart and a new spirit with a new awareness of the reality of what he calls 'eschatological forgiveness'. That is the forgiveness which finally resolves both sin and its consequences. The making real of this forgiveness was to become one of the key elements of the new order. God must transform human society to reflect justice, righteousness and peace. And he must transform nature itself to get rid of hunger, disease, and all that makes human life less than safe or desirable, and so to establish a new natural order in which lions can lie down with lambs (Isaiah 11:6–9). This can only happen as a result of God's initiative. The centre of this activity will be Zion. But the catalyst for it will be a divine agent.

Reflection on Text

If you read **Ezekiel 36:22–38** you will get a sense of the new mood about the future, and the need for fundamental change. Is there anything here that you would recognize as relevant to our own day? If you had to make a list of things that need to change what would it look like? Would they be the kinds of thing that could be changed by human activity? If some of them are not, how does it feel to recognize that there are some things which cannot be achieved in that way?

Enter (and Exit) Jesus

There is little scholarly agreement on what was definitely believed about this divine agent and his activity by the time of Jesus. Certainly, three key terms are: kingdom of God, Messiah and Son of Man. There are resonances, in the hopes expressed through these terms of a restoration, of the best aspects of the original Israelite monarchy of God's first Messiah, his first anointed one, David. Hopes of unity, reconciliation, peace, justice and plenty are all associated with David's rule in Jerusalem. Alongside these hopes is a growing concern for the vindication, the public 'proving right' of those who have remained faithful against all the odds, the remnant. A famous passage in Daniel 7:13 describes how this group is presented to the Ancient of Days for vindication by 'one like a Son of Man'. Precisely what part this text played in interpreting contemporary religious life by the time of Jesus is disputed. What is clear is that in times of enormous political instability, eschatology came to be the dominant theological mode. People of faith lived by their hope in God's ability and imminent desire to change things for the better. The worse things got, the more important became the need for intervention and change. The more experience contradicted faith, and the more God appeared to be absent and uninterested, the more pressing was the need for some new sighting of God, some kind of evidence that he was still around and interested. For people who were suffering, the problem of evil was the key theological problem, and it needed to be dealt with. Reading the New Testament Gospels in particular we can sense deep religious anxiety. The stakes are high. Is Jesus the one who is to come, or should people be looking for someone else? becomes a key question. The Christian claim is that Jesus is indeed the Messiah, the promised one, but . . . and it's a very big but. Jesus is Son of God, no less, but not as we know it. The first three Gospel writers are unanimous that Jesus calls himself Son of Man, and that his main message is about the nearness of the kingdom of God. But he suffers and dies. That is not how the script should run for someone about to change the course of world history in God's name.

And so, the Christian claims about Jesus are all the more remarkable, because they precipitate exactly the kind of crisis which the Old Testament Exile represented. On the face of it that seems like an odd claim. The people of New Testament times were not conquered, deported or made to suffer physically. But just as the Old Testament Exile had meant that firm expectations of God had not been met, and so the rug of meaning that people depended upon had been pulled from beneath them, so the Christian claim that God had been crucified could only lead to confusion and disbelief. For the second time in the Judaeo-Christian tradition this is where religion should have ended.

Jürgen Moltmann puts it at its bluntest: 'Faith in the crucified God is . . . a contradiction of everything men have ever conceived, denied and sought to be assured of by the term "God".'[8] It was not possible in the theological vocabulary and imagination of the time to be God and yet suffer and die. The only options for faith appear to be either to give in to atheism, admitting that the whole religion thing was a cruel delusion, opium for the masses; or else to work out what kind of redefinition of religion could possibly make sense of that which conviction born of experience demanded. A third option was to deny that Jesus was the Christ at all. This could be seen as the sensible option which is represented by those who observed Jesus on the cross, and replay the Christians' claims about him in a way which makes them seem ludicrous. 'Those who passed by derided him, shaking their heads and saying, "He saved others; he cannot save himself. He is the king of Israel; let him come down from the cross now, and we will believe in him"' (Matthew 27:42). It is part of the Gospel writers' art that we are left unsympathetic towards these sentiments, just as we are left unsympathetic towards the demands for demonstration of messiahship made by the devil (Matthew 4:1–11), or the careful questioning of the Pharisees designed to establish just who Jesus is, despite the fact that really they are quite understandable. As readers of the Gospels we are being asked to accept as normal and real something which is quite surreal and contradicts our usual reading of reality.

Reflection on Text

Imagine yourself as a devout religious person, around the time of Jesus, who has really taken seriously the prevailing religious mood that God is about to intervene directly in human affairs. Try to imagine how you would feel at the time of the crucifixion. Which response is most understandable – that of **Matthew 27:42** or that of **Matthew 27:54**? How do you account for the difference between them?

The response to the crisis also mirrors that of the time of Exile, at least from a Christian perspective. This becomes a second new time of theological creativity. Christian writers work from the premise that they had not known as much about God as they thought they had, and that what they had seen in Jesus was an authentic and further revelation which demanded new thinking. Just as at the time of the Exile, we now see the response of creative and dynamic faith in New Testament documents which suggest new definitions of identity, new ways of being religious and a retelling of the story so far, so that it accords with the present facts rather than contradicts them. Jesus is the Son of Man/Son of David/Messiah/ but not as we know it. This is the Kingdom of Heaven but not as we expect it. There is a way of maintaining faith in God and being religious with integrity even in these new times, and it's a way which is even more realistic because it has at its heart the key issue of suffering. But just how close are the parallels between the Old Testament exilic theological enterprise and this one?

Brueggemann believes they are very close and that new light can be shed on the New Testament story of crucifixion and resurrection by considering them in the light of the Exile.[9] But does the New Testament itself reflect this view? That will depend to some extent on what we consider the main characteristics of 'exilic' theology to be. Our enquiries have shown that the major crisis to which this theology reacts is of uncertainty about a God one thought one knew. The religious life had been about responding to this God in a way which would guarantee final vindication or salvation. At the time of the Exile, religious people experienced abandonment by this God and a subsequent sense of uncertainty about vindication. The earliest New Testament theology we have, that of Paul, certainly reflects this theme. One could almost call it his basic theme. Although he makes no overt reference to the time of Exile, the theology he devises for the present crisis could in our sense be called 'exilic'.

Paul and the Crucified God

He explains that the cross signals an end to the old way of understanding God, vindication and salvation. The cross is an annulment of what religious people expect from God, and there can be no denial option. There is no letting God off the hook. Paul's first task is to assert that Jesus did suffer and die, and that is not just an illusion as some later heretics might want to claim. Romans 4:25 tells us Jesus was 'handed over to death'; Romans 5:8, that while we were still sinners 'Christ died for us'. And it wasn't just that he died, though that might have been taken as the ultimate proof of his 'non-divinity'. The manner of his death is detailed. 'I decided to know nothing among you except Jesus Christ, and him crucified' (1 Corinthians 2:2). 'He humbled himself and became obedient to the point of death – even death on a cross' (Philippians 2:8). Consequently, Christ became a curse for us since: 'cursed is everyone who hangs on a tree' (Galatians 3:13) and 'He made him to be sin who knew no sin' (2 Corinthians 5:21). No one according to the old dispensation can be both sin and God, since sin is by definition that which is not God. Paul is stating outright that the first effect of the cross must be to change our concept of God. The cross signals the end of the old God – the God of common religion – the God to whom we can appeal to change things. Our concept of God must now include that *as part of his nature* God can suffer and can identify completely with humanity without loss of Godness by becoming sin and by becoming a curse.

In terms reminiscent of exilic theology, Paul takes up the case of the God who appears to promise and then fail. His ideas are not set in the form of a contrived novel like Job, but he does engage in a kind of dialogue with the various traditions by which people articulated their hope of deliverance.

Paul in 1 Corinthians 2:2 signals his determination to test all of these traditions in the light of the cross. The Messiah, the great white hope, as it were, has come and has been crucified. Therefore either hope or *messiahship* needs to be redefined. Those who hope that by keeping *the law* they will be vindicated also find little comfort in Paul. Romans 10:4 tells us that 'Christ is the end of the law', and Colossians 2:14 illustrates this end graphically: '. . . erasing the record that stood against us with its legal demands . . . he set this aside, nailing it to the cross'. The search for *wisdom* will not bring vindication, since in traditional terms the cross is the ultimate in folly (1 Corinthians 1:18ff.). What people want from God is demonstrable *power*. What they actually get is the exact opposite (2 Corinthians 11:30, 13:4). In summary, the ideas of the whole religious world are turned on their heads by a crucified Christ, 'a stumbling block to Jews and foolishness to Gentiles' (1 Corinthians 1:23). Just as God intended the Exile, so God intended the abuse and crucifixion of Jesus. They are part of the puzzle of God; not evidence against God.

The exilic theological response was one which understood the new experiences to point to something more wondrous about God than had been formerly imagined.

Paul's response is in exactly these terms as we see him redefining faith. Under the old understanding, faith is essentially a human act, made in response to God's demands in the hope of final vindication. The radical redefinition of faith which Paul describes involves seeing faith as primarily God's act resulting from God's initiative. In this, the whole idea of vindication is turned upside down. In the Old Testament vindication was described in terms of ascent (Daniel 7:13), people are brought up to God. The vindication which Paul describes is in terms of descent – God comes down to us. And that is not a spatial descent from heaven to earth, but a qualitative descent from power to weakness. God's taking the initiative is God's 'keeping faith' and in fact this is the only important act of faith for salvation. ('What if some were unfaithful? Will their faithlessness nullify the faithfulness of God? By no means!' Romans 3:3.) God is the epitome of faithfulness (1 Thessalonians 5:14). In Paul's vocabulary of salvation, faith and grace predicated of God amount to the same thing, evidenced in Christ, God's ultimate act of faith. The scheme of salvation amounts to this: humanity is justified by God's faith in us; exemplified in the graceful stooping, lowering, friend-making action of sending his Son. 'Justification by Faith' on any other terms is an obvious nonsense. The appropriate human response is the humble one of accepting that this is the case – that Jesus Christ is God's act of justifying grace. Ephesians 2:8 sums it up: 'For by grace you have been saved through faith; and this is not your own doing, it is the gift of God.'

This is a potentially subversive corrective to a majority religious view which sees faith as a pious act with a human subject. Faith, according to Paul is almost coextensive with incarnation, has God as its subject, and itself needs to be revealed. The revelation of faith or the coming of Christ is proof of God's having justified us, a proof which enables us to be sons and heirs of God (Galatians 3:23f.). On this view (and this is what makes it dangerous) there is no reciprocal act that human beings can make towards God corresponding to God's act of faith in us that can be instrumental in our own salvation. That is also why it leads to a view of God which is 'bigger' than that which preceded it. Accepting the gift with good grace becomes the touchstone of Christian living.

The eschatological hopes of transformation are not annulled in Paul's understanding of the scheme of things. Romans, chapter 8:20f. reiterates the theme, but there is now no scheme for the future by which God's success will be judged. It might be said that pre-cross eschatology had systematized history and almost made God a prisoner to the system in much the same way that pre-exilic theology had made God prisoner to systems and rules. Paul argues for a degree of agnosticism about the future ('hope that is seen is not hope' (Romans 8:24), but maintains belief in the possibilities of God with regard to the future. Just as exilic theologians needed to reiterate that faith means trust, so Paul reasserts that hope means trust. Romans 5:1–5 shows the close relationship between faith and hope; and that God's act of faith in us is what gives ground to the trust and makes hope a realistic option.

Further evidence that for Paul relationship is more important than system, is provided by his emphasis on love. The act of becoming weak, the being prepared to suffer, the laying of oneself open vulnerably are all evidence of God's love for us. That we should be thought worth it is almost inconceivable, and this is how the transcendence of God is now understood. These are better demonstrations of God's essential nature than any number of so-called powerful displays might have been (Romans 5:8, 8:39; 2 Corinthians 5:14). The Christian life must imitate this love, which means, practically, that it must opt for weakness in preference to power (2 Corinthians 11:30, 13:4). We are no longer cast as people who can only be persuaded to do other than we naturally wish by the promise of vindication in some other realm. We now live in the awareness of being seriously loved. The implication is that Christian ministry must reflect this love to others. In fact Paul sometimes uses the same word-root (*charis*, *charizo*) to express both God's act of grace towards us, and the appropriate way for us to deal with others. This is not usually apparent from the English translation (compare Colossians 3:13, 16, 4:5). Such love is not to be confined to personal acts and relationships. It is essentially manifested in communal terms (1 Corinthians 14:1) where it can be described as *koinonia* or fellowship, sharing and participation. This idea is also connected with worship. The cup and bread of the Eucharist are both a *koinonia* of the body and blood of Christ (1 Corinthians 10:16f.).

Paul could therefore be said to mirror the post-exilic theological enterprise in that he:

- Identifies a fundamental disjunction between old and new forms of being religious;
- Recognizes that this spells a crisis for religion;
- Redefines the meaning of salvation, according to a conviction born of new experience;
- Rediscovers more wondrous things about God;
- Finds (like Job) a sighting and audition of God in the midst of the crisis, enabling statements about faith and hope in terms of relationships rather than systems;
- Sets out the implications for worship, communal religious identity and the life and behaviour of believers;
- Seems to commend a new sense of openness and freedom to a world-view characterized by closedness and anxiety.

Exiles and Aliens

But having said all of this, there is little or no overt reference to the Exile in the generally recognized writings of

Paul. He writes as one unaware in this respect of the tradition in which he stands, though that in itself need not disqualify him from this discussion.

Overt references to the Old Testament Exile in the New Testament are very few and far between. Matthew's genealogy (Matthew 1:11f.) describes it as one of the major divisions of traditional history. It is all the more strange, in that case, that it then disappears from sight. At least, the inclusion of the Exile in such a scheme enables us to say that the Exile was considered as theologically significant, and in so far as this is some kind of recital of the history of salvation it is surely significant that it contrived in such a way that the Exile is a pivotal part of it and the Exodus is not mentioned at all. This could be seen, though, as an attempt, like those of D and P, to give the history of the people of God a new frame of reference. Like those Old Testament works it does this not by telling the story as if the past hadn't mattered but by trying to make credible links between what was known and what is now experienced. Matthew continues to do this as he draws on 'proof texts' to strengthen arguments at significant points in his Gospel.

Reflection on Text

Read **Matthew 1:1–17**. It may be that you have always skipped over this bit of the Gospel before. Now read it carefully and see if you can find:

- References to famous men from the Old Testament;
- References to famous women from the Old Testament;
- Reference as to how history is to be divided.

Thinking about your lists, how does this section of text help to tell us who Jesus is?

Exiles are mentioned in three other places, in all of which the Babylonian Exile presumably provides the model. We shall look at Ephesians 2:11–22 and Hebrews 11:13–16 briefly in the next chapter. But by far the most interesting remaining document is 1 Peter.

Not long ago 1 Peter was described as the 'storm centre of New Testament studies', on the grounds that conclusions about its nature and purpose were among the most disputed within New Testament scholarship.[10] Although scholarship is still far from unanimous, there is a growing consensus that the work is pseudonymous, that it belongs to the period 70–90 CE; that the communities addressed are undergoing some kind of local harassment on account of their being Christians, and that some traditional materials such as creeds and codes have been incorporated into the text. The addressees live in what would now be called western Turkey, in scattered rural areas adjacent to those addressed in the New Testament Apocalypse at roughly the same time as that latter document might have been written. They clearly belong to the servant rather than the master social class and one is struck from the outset by the experience of weakness, vulnerability, and perhaps abandonment, which has prompted the letter. Most importantly for our present purpose, they are described as exiles of the dispersion (1 Peter 1:1).

This is no superficial reference. In fact two different Greek words are used to describe the condition of the addressees. One means more specifically 'exiles' while the other means something like 'resident aliens'. The two terms are often used together (as at 2:11, compare Genesis 23:4) and could be said to be almost interchangeable. If we regard them as such we could see that the theological context of 1 Peter 1:1 is repeated at 1:17 ('the time of your exile') and 2:11 ('I urge you as aliens and exiles'). There is also a reference in 5:13 to Babylon, here as elsewhere in the writings of late antiquity presumably referring to Rome. The letter is addressed to a situation which is perceived by those who are part of it to be one of suffering. I put it thus because scholars are undecided about the severity of the suffering, or its authors. However, in relation to its length, 1 Peter contains more reference to suffering than does any other book of the New Testament and it seems fair to conclude that from a subjective standpoint suffering was happening. There is a parallel with the Exile here, in that scholars also debate the severity of the suffering of the Old Testament exiles. The point there, as in 1 Peter, is that the severity is not necessarily the issue. It is what the suffering represents in terms of structures of meaning which is important. The only really important thing is that the experiences of the people, in both cases, are experienced as *significant*. It is this suffering which the author chooses to describe as in the context of exile.

There are other similarities between the Old Testament exiles and those in 1 Peter. In both cases there is a sense of God's having withdrawn. If the date is right, then these are communities that have every right to be concerned. The first flush of Christian enthusiasm was over. The great writers and speakers were dead as, by and large, were those who knew them. Christianity was regarded with suspicion by just about everybody. The state thought it could be subversive. Jews were anxious not to be associated with this new sect for fear of losing hard-won privileges in the Roman empire. In terms of the hopes for a new world order, little if anything had changed, and certainly nothing had changed for the better. Nothing had happened to give further credibility to Christian claims about transformation. The first Christian holocaust, under Nero, seemed to point to the shape of things to come. These were not great times to be a Christian despite the attempts of Luke to persuade us otherwise. (It is a tremendous tribute to his presentation skills that at the end of the Acts of the Apostles we can be left wondering, how could it all be so successful? when as we can see from reading between the lines elsewhere, many were wondering if the whole thing was doomed to failure.) A new sighting of God was urgently needed.

We do have a sense in 1 Peter of a community at odds with its context. Quite simply, they do not feel as if they *belong*. John Elliott has developed a thesis about the social strategy of the book which begins from this point.[11] Research into the socio-political context of first-century Asia Minor suggests that the Greek term *paroikoi,* has a technical sense of 'resident aliens' akin to asylum-seekers perhaps in Britain, or more precisely, Turkish guest-workers in Germany. They have permission to be where they are but they are not citizens and there is nothing permanent or guaranteed about their continuing there. They are at the most vulnerable end of society, blamed for most of its ills, and constantly living under threat. This too, perhaps gives some definition to the force of the address as exiles.

A third point of resonance is that the letter betrays a sense of something fundamental and significant just having happened in the lives of the addressees that calls for further commentary and exploration. The letter has a very strong sense of beginnings and endings. The usual way with commentators is to relate this entirely to baptism – about which 1 Peter has more to say than most New Testament writings – but baptism is itself a shorthand for the fundamental changes which have happened. In any case it is notable that in describing baptism 1 Peter uses the image of the water that drowns rather than that which cleanses (3:21). Baptism is a kind of death. A fundamental disjunction has occurred. Other references to this fundamental shift include: 1:3 (new birth), 1:14 (your former desires), 1:18 (you were ransomed), 1:23 (you have been born anew), 2:2 (like newborn infants), 2:10 (once you were no people; now you are God's people), 3:6 (you have become daughters of Sarah), 4:2 (live no longer by human desires), and 4:3f. (no longer living like Gentiles). So what does the document have to say to these people, who are exiles in the sense that they experience suffering, they don't belong, they have undergone a fundamental and significant shift with implications for meaning in their lives and who are experiencing God's absence?

Just as the post-exilic theologians retell the story of the community of faith in a way which takes account of present circumstances and includes the addressees as part of it, so the author of 1 Peter is keen to reassure his readers that the Old Testament epithets of chosenness still apply to them. They are chosen, destined, sanctified and ransomed. They are a holy priesthood, a chosen race, a royal priesthood, a holy nation and God's own people. But in order to make that claim stick, just as in Old Testament theology, or with Paul, the author of 1 Peter has to redefine some of those epithets in a way which would render them unrecognizable to those for whom they originally had meaning. This is a mixed-race group, so how can they be a chosen race or a holy nation? Priesthood and royalty are both exclusive terms. How can they possibly be appropriate to this disparate group of lower-class aliens. The temple is a fixed religious institution. How can the company of believers supersede it?

Perhaps the greatest contribution of 1 Peter and the most adventurous flight of fancy from this exile, is the redefinition of the religious establishment in these deeply ironic terms. Now, the whole company of believers can in principle do what hitherto was only possible for people from a special caste within a special nation in a special place at a special time in a special way. This points to a whole new way of being religious and firmly places 1 Peter in the tradition of exilic theology. Other responses are also familiar. The letter includes a large number of apocalyptic sentiments, language forms and ideas. For those who are asking, 'how long?' in this new situation of suffering, the answer about a God who has planned all this and who is just on the verge of revealing his hand is congenial. But there is a new answer here too. The suffering of believers is combined in some mystical way with that of Christ.

In part, this is a way of saying that suffering is redemptive. The language of Isaiah 53 is employed to remind the sufferers that Jesus' suffering was for a purpose. In part it is an appeal to take heart from the model of suffering which Jesus provided. He has shared that experience with us. He knows what it's like. This has huge pastoral power. The writer goes to great lengths to identify the suffering of believers with that of Jesus. Many words are used in 1 Peter that are only used elsewhere in the New Testament in the Gospel passion narratives. To become a Christian is almost, then, to expect and sign up to suffering. The links in literature of this period between baptism, martyrdom and death seem to point in this same direction. But there is something more than this and something new. It is not just that Jesus is sharing our sufferings. By suffering we are sharing his sufferings. Our suffering *is* his suffering (4:13).

This point is not unique to the author of 1 Peter. In fact Paul makes much of it too, but it is notable that in both cases, this daring new assertion about God and the believer should come from the tradition of doing theology set by the Exile. In fact what we see is that suffering becomes the dominant mode of expression for Christianity and its distinctive and definitive voice. This means that from now on, not only can almost all theological axioms be expressed in terms of suffering, but also that experiences and contexts of suffering give best indications for sightings and auditions of God.

Reflection on Experience

Think of a time when you have been aware of suffering that has been so intolerable that you have been prompted to ask questions such as: Why does God allow this? Think back to the kinds of answer to that question given by Job's friends. How much difference does it make or would it make to think of God, not as *sending* suffering but *sharing* it? How satisfying a notion is it to you that the church might be called to share Christ's sufferings in the world? Can you think of an example where that could happen or is happening? On September 11, 2001 could you have answered the question: Where is God in all this? in terms of his being in the midst of the suffering and sharing it? Would your view of God have to change to allow that?

Conclusion

Thus, hugely creative theological ideas, subversive as far as the old religious order would be concerned, have emerged from a situation in which, according to those old rules, religion and faith in God should have died. As the result of a huge crisis which had fundamental significance for those involved, there is a redefinition of faith, of the religious community (and by implication of the pastoral task) of worship, and of the way we understand God. This came from a situation which those at the heart of it could describe in terms of suffering and displacement. It was achieved against the odds and the vested interests of those who wanted to believe that things could continue as if nothing had happened. It's another example of the exile process.

5

Tourists, Ex-Pats and Other Strangers

Introduction

For the Christian today, to leave home can be a bewildering ideological challenge. Are you going as a tourist or a pilgrim? Will you be a guest or a stranger? Is it the journey that's important or the destination? Is there some commitment built into the journey so that it will somehow help to change things back home or not? Anyone who doubts the importance of these questions need only read *Beyond Theological Tourism*, in which Susan Thistlethwaite and George Cairns (among others) help define what's at stake in these various descriptions, in order to be persuaded.[12] So what kind of journey is involved today in an *exile*, and how does that relate to these other kinds of travel, if at all?

Our review of the biblical record has given us ample evidence of why scholars are finding something new and exciting in this way of reading the texts. It has also helped define more closely what I think we need to learn from that record as we try to assess what it has to teach us about appropriate modes of church life for today. We have spoken of an 'exilic process'. This is a process which can be seen at work in response both to the Old Testament Exile and the New Testament crucifixion, and which is largely responsible for the written Testaments we have and the theology they contain. The process operates principally in response to situations that are perceived to constitute crises for faith and that appear to give fresh evidence of God's absence or even further evidence of the stupidity of belief in God and any consequent religious activity. But, as we have noted in passing, this is not the only way, or even the majority way in which the idea or metaphor of exile is applied.

Babylon

Throughout Christian history, the term 'Babylon' has been a helpful one for those writers who have wished to denounce true Christianity's enemies. The New Testament book of Revelation gives examples of this, projecting the hostile power aspect of Babylon on to Rome (see, for example: 14:8, 16:19, 17:5, 18:2, 10, 21). Later, Augustine was to use the metaphor of Babylon as the prototype of the earthly city of death and confusion (*City of God*: 18.42). Dante was among those who opposed the sojourn of the papacy in Avignon (1309–77) and regarded it as the Babylonian captivity of the papacy. In 1520 Luther's *Babylonian Captivity of the Church* used the same metaphor to denounce the sacramental theology of the Roman Church. In each of these cases there is little to connect them with the sixth-century BCE Exile as such. The metaphor is recognized as a pervasive one, which has more general resonances with the human condition. David Reimer makes two points worth noting. First: 'Clearly the symbol of alienation is at the forefront of Christian usage of the metaphor of exile'; and second: 'Use of the language of exile commonly neglects the aspect of restoration.'[13] Our use of 'exilic process' expressly includes the restoration, and indeed the later dispersion, insofar as they are contexts for reflection on the events of exile.

Kinds of Exile

So the most usual use of the term 'exile' denotes someone who is estranged from their homeland. This exile can either be enforced, as for example in the case of refugees from war or disaster, or a matter of choice. I myself am an exile in this latter sense. I was born a Yorkshireman but I have spent a large part of my life in Wales, a country with a different culture and language. As I write, I am visiting New Zealand in a kind of self-imposed exile which places me in a new and unfamiliar context. I can use this shorthand for estrangement in other personal ways. For example, I was brought up as a Methodist but am now an Anglican. It is thus possible to describe objectively a wide variety of changes in my life in terms of exile. To do so might be to make the assumption that the original always had priority; that the land of my birth will always be my homeland however much I feel at home in another. Or, it could be that the term 'exile' only has real force when I *feel* estrangement. The Welsh word *hiraeth*, loosely translated 'longing' might be thought the appropriate mode of exilic perception in these circumstances. *Hiraeth* is something more than the kind of nostalgia which inhabits most of us at sometime for things that are gone, never to return, but exiles may experience both nostalgia and *hiraeth*.

Reflection on Experience

Try to remember (or if you took them you could refer to any notes you made) your response to the first reflection on experience in Chapter 1, in which you were invited to think about what it means to be an exile. Having had a chance to look in more detail at biblical texts and think more deeply about the issues raised, do you want to revise your initial estimate in any way?

Or it could be that in order to make connections with the biblical understanding of exile there needs to be some element of hardship. Ex-pats are often thought to have opted for their status in order to have a relatively comfortable life with enhanced tax breaks, higher standards of living and a more luxurious lifestyle. They are exiles in an objective sense, and from time to time may experience bouts of nostalgia or even the deep longing of *hiraeth*, but is it fair to compare them with those for whom the move to exile has been deeply traumatic? On the other hand, there are those who have experienced deep trauma which has marked such a significant stage in their lives that it might almost be called an end and a new beginning; a death and a new life, but which has not necessarily moved them spatially at all. Or again, are the language and ideas about exile simply a convenient way of marking afresh the alternative nature of Christian life? Are they a way of saying that Christians will always feel like strangers in a world which does not hold their values? This is the implication of Hebrews 11:13–16. Christians, or people of faith, will always be strangers and feel like exiles on earth because their true citizenship is in heaven. That is the only place where their values are honoured and affirmed.

It is interesting that the Greek word for 'church' that we find in the New Testament – *ecclesia* (which gives us the English word 'ecclesiastical' or the Welsh word *eglwys*) develops quickly in post-New Testament times to mean the universal church, or the concept of church. The word *paroikia*, which we have come across in 1 Peter, meaning 'resident aliens', is the word increasingly used to describe an individual church settlement, and eventually reaches the English language in the word 'parish'. On a straightforward reading, a parish is a settlement of resident aliens whose true citizenship is in heaven.

Reflection on Experience

If you have had experience of a Christian church, does the idea of a community church as a gathering of 'resident aliens' make any sense to you? How would any church you know have to change, in order for this description to fit, do you think?

Ephesians, chapter 2 uses the idea in a different way. Here the Gentiles' former life is described using the language of exile. But now these people have, as it were, come home. They are no longer strangers and aliens. They are citizens of the household of God (Ephesians 2:19). Elliott's interpretation of 1 Peter reaches similar conclusions. For him, the strategy of the book is to assure these people of apparently little worth in the citizenship stakes; these people who are at the bottom of the pile in terms of identity; these homeless; that they do indeed have a home. They are part of the household of God (1 Peter 4:17), and more importantly, stones within a spiritual house (1 Peter 2:5). In both these cases the interpretation would lead to the view that *settledness* is the appropriate mode of church life. Life as an exile for the addressees was abnormal and temporary. Now citizenship has given them something permanent, but alternative. The Hebrews passage takes a different view, namely that *restlessness* is the appropriate mode of church life on this earth. The eventual promised Sabbath rest is part of the eschatological hope. Perhaps settledness and restlessness are not as mutually exclusive as they seem. Perhaps there is a way of describing the life of faith in terms of temporary settledness; a settledness that has a larger context of restlessness; a settledness which recognizes that there is need for further resolution. Perhaps we could describe this way of life, using Klein's phrase, as a settledness that sees itself as 'our home for the time being'.[14]

Reflection on Text

Read **Ephesians 2** and **Hebrews 11:13–16**. Do you recognize the distinction made above? Is restlessness or settledness the more attractive in terms of how you see church life developing?

Modern Applications

It is important for us to know what kinds of situation make legitimate connection, pastorally, with exile theology. Is it only important in the camps of the West Bank, or could it be applied to those in America trying to make sense of the events of September 11? Can it be applied to those who are faced with some personal tragedy such as the death of a child, or is it a way of helping people write a commentary on the many non-traumatic changes and developments in their lives? Is it something which is only appropriate for churches to consider in their relations with the wider world, or is it an appropriate category for the analysis of world events and social changes? Some recent treatments of the theme provide pointers.

Stanley Hauerwas and William H. Willimon use the title *Resident Aliens* for a work published in 1989.[15] Their biblical starting point is Philippians 3:20, 'our commonwealth is in heaven', and they understand the church to be in exile insofar as it represents a Christian colony of heaven on alien soil. They do write in response to what they see as a crucial shift in their world, which they fear too few from the churches have noticed, but which is represented for them by the Sunday opening of cinemas in formerly Bible-belt areas. They fear that, in an American context, the church has bought too readily into a liberal agenda which historically left it theologically powerless to defy Nazism or the bombing of Hiroshima, and which is now content to see itself colluding with American culture rather than challenging it. Hence their appeal is for a new theological understanding of the church, an ecclesiology. 'We would like a church that again asserts that God, not nations, rules the world, that the boundaries of God's kingdom transcend those of Caesar, and that the main political task of the church is the formation of people who see clearly the cost of discipleship and are willing to pay the price'.[16]

They believe that the predominant ethos of church life in America is Constantinian (that is 'established' and state sanctioned) and want to describe church life in a way that relates to heaven rather than the state (using the Philippians language). So their emphasis is on life in the Christian colony, concentrating particularly on how a Christian understanding of life is to be passed on to the next generation. This is, of course, always a key indicator of how a church understands what Christian life is going to be about from now on. Interestingly, the centre of this is a mentoring programme which will have 'an ability to bring generations of disciples together'.[17] These authors are particularly deprecating about ministerial training, which they believe has not taken account of the changed world, in which the ethical bases of the state have diverged so markedly from those of Christianity, and which still prepares for citizenship of America rather than colonist status in the church. They have doubts about whether serving the world, in the way it is understood by seminaries, is a genuinely Christian task, and believe there should be more obvious distance between the life of the church and American society's materialism. They note the large number of disillusioned clergy, and pour scorn on attempts to help them in terms of improving their conditions. What they need is a new and adventurous sense of theology.

Whilst we may agree wholeheartedly and enthusias-tically that the problem for many clergy is that they were not inspired at their training colleges with sustainable theological tools which would equip them for adventurous and fulfilling ministry throughout their lifetimes, that need not lead us to the view of church life proposed. *Resident Aliens* has little to say about exile other than using the term to highlight the seriousness and urgency with which the authors see the need for churches to work at ecclesiology a bit more and sociology a bit less. My view is that the exilic process will itself provide a way of understanding what the church is and what it might be for, that will be exciting and adventurous, without leading in what looks suspiciously like a sectarian direction. In fairness, the American context of fifteen years ago is far removed from our context now, but that only serves to highlight the need for something more local and immediate.

There is further opportunity to see how Willimon's ideas have developed in a collection called *Good News in Exile,* published in 1999.[18] To read this book is to have the distinct feeling of intruding on private grief. All the contributors grew up with a set of assumptions about Christianity's relationship with civic American life which have now been shattered. Neither their upbringing nor their theological education prepared them for what they now perceive ministry to demand. This too, then, is a book which uses the idea of exile to describe a divergence between church and society in America. In the foreword Walter Brueggemann defines his understanding of how they use the term 'exile' as: 'a context of doing faith in an environment that is variously hostile or indifferent to that faith'.[19] Insofar as exile itself gets a mention in the book it is used in connection with a rediscovery of scripture. This is now to be seen as 'our home in exile' suggested by Brueggemann's observation that in the Old Testament Exile the people of Israel became a textual community for the first time and sustained themselves with stories that declared who they were. This new home in exile frees people from unfettered individualism, which would otherwise be their fate.

This adds little to the previous discussion, apart from the suggestion of hostility or indifference in the environment. The world has undoubtedly changed for these writers, and it has changed in a way that raises fundamental issues of meaning and which questions held assumptions. It has forced them to look at what religion is in a new way, and has pushed them in the theological direction of ecclesiology. All this fits within an exilic frame and yet . . . the conclusions they reach are all about the church rather than the world, or human destiny, or any grand design. Brueggemann's assertion about the exilic community as a textual community implies far more than they appear to suspect. The end result still seems rather staid and unlikely to inspire future generations of American Christians in the way intended. Rather than giving an adventurous opportunity to reassess the grandeur of God we see something that looks much more like a rearguard regrouping with a very limited agenda. Writing, as I am, in a state which is secular to an extent I have not previously encountered; and attempting to celebrate Christmas in the unfamiliar surroundings of a country where there is no religious teaching or consequent nativity plays in schools; with scant acknowledgement of religion in the public media, I am more aware than ever of how easy it is to dismiss public religion. And so I am more wary than I might otherwise have been about a view like Willimon's which is so bound up with a particular American context.

Reflection on Experience

Can you think of times when you have felt that the church was too easily accepting the values and priorities of the state? How do you feel about the following?

- Remembrance Sunday Services
- Services in church for secular organizations
- Christmas Eve communion services

What do you think churches ought to be protesting to the state most vigorously about? If you do this as a group exercise it will be interesting to see what measure of agreement there is.

Walter Brueggemann's own work is of a different order. In *Cadences of Home*, he states that his purpose is not primarily institutional but pastoral, that is he wants to explore how 'the exiles experienced a loss of the structured reliable world which gave them meaning and coherence'. Exile, he says, 'is not primarily geographical, but it is social moral and cultural'.[20] The links he makes from this are with a culture in which Christians are at odds with their capitalist environment, and with the changes that are being brought about in society, as the white male-dominated, western models are being increasingly questioned. Exile, for him, from this pastoral perspective, is characterized by honest sadness, a sense of abandonment, a tendency to despair which is recovered by prophetic words of hope, questioning about the moral coherence of life, and a pre-occupation with self. His work is well supported with biblical evidence but essentially and overtly related also to an American context. Brueggemann's characterization of the marks of exile is one that we can recognize and be excited by. He outlines a pastoral task in which the human conditions he has identified are met with biblical resources.

Brueggemann also contributes a foreword to another

recent treatment of the theme by Daniel Smith-Christopher. He notes with approval Smith-Christopher's arguments that 'invite a rethinking and repositioning of church in US society'.[21] So far this sounds like familiar territory. However, there are some new contributions. The author takes issue with some recent (mostly British) scholarship which is sceptical about the historical veracity of the Exile. As we have seen he counters it not only with biblical arguments but by reference to refugee and disaster studies, and work on post-traumatic stress disorder, showing a consonance between those studies and the evidence in biblical texts. He is particularly keen to see *actual* suffering taken into account in the application of any exile paradigm. Some of this concern derives from his having spent time in Palestine as a member of a 'peace church', and he is also particularly concerned about theologies of power, especially after September 11, 2001, which attempt to find biblical warrant for war. He believes exilic or diaspora theology is post-colonial, peace-oriented and contextual. This is a mature and thoughtful contribution to the task of redefining the role of the church in relation to American society. Like Willimon and Brueggemann, this work acknowledges its debt to the work of John Howard Yoder, which gives an indication of the main likely direction of the results, in terms of the relationship between politics and religion.

Mention might also be made of an older study by Ralph Klein, *Israel in Exile: A Theological Interpretation*.[22] Klein sees a wide-ranging application for exilic theology. On the one hand he sees the institutional problem of the church's proper response to social and political crises such as war and the exhaustion of energy resources. However he does not take the view of Willimon, and sees 'no call away from the struggle for social justice and world peace'. As in Jeremiah's time, 'We need to seek the peace of this city, to pray for our enemy's prosperity, to know that here and now is the arena of our vocation.'[23] He also sees a more individual application of the theology. 'For us too, the old answers no longer hold; our optimistic expectations are contradicted by our increasingly depressing experiences. One can be in exile without ever leaving the land.'[24] Much of his interest, in this context, is centred on the response of the theologian and Old-Testament writers of the P school in the old Testament.

Exile and Church

In response to this work, I am least persuaded by those who wish to press the institutional application of this theology, in the sense of defining the church's relation to other social institutions, civic or national. This has the effect, for me, of trivializing the plight of those who are even today experiencing real suffering in real exile and trying to make sense of what the community of faith might mean in the midst of it. To claim that in any such sense America is experiencing something that could be described as exile seems to me to be the equivalent of going into a West Bank refugee camp and saying: 'I know exactly how you feel, as a Yorkshireman living in Wales. I don't know when I last had proper Yorkshire pudding or decent fish and chips.' I am most persuaded by those who want at least to begin from the pastoral application. In other words I do not believe that for the most part the church in the western world is *in exile*. I *do* think that it might usefully be considered as being *a place for exiles*. However, that is not to dismiss the approach of Willimon. In fact I agree with him that the chief pastoral contribution we need to make at this time is the provision of a theology of the church. I also agree with Brueggemann that this needs to be done in the context of a genuine conversation, and with Klein that the resulting process will need to take full account of, amongst others, the theological exilic response of P.

Willimon complains that, when the traditional church

edifice is crumbling, no one seems to know what the church is for any more. He sees that the churches meet this with an ever more frenzied series of social programmes. One can only sympathize with such an arid experience of church life, and agree that what is most urgently needed is a response which does attempt to set out what church is for, that is, an ecclesiology; and why it might all be worth it, that is, a theology. Other elements of church life will result from this. It will be those understandings which give point to worship, focus to ministry and rationale to church involvement in the world outside itself. My point of divergence with Willimon is that it might then seem to an observer that the church which has undergone this process will still be as passionately committed to social programmes as it was hitherto; might still be as involved in civic life, and still in a position to influence the activities of the state. To assume otherwise from the outset, seems to me to assume that the church will always be a minority within society and always at odds with its environment, and I see no biblical warrant for that.

The first important thing, then, is that the theological response is made, and that it starts from a pastoral application. To say that the pastoral application needs to be understood in terms of theology is to deny any definition of 'pastoral' that distinguishes between theology and pastoralia. One might equally well speak of a theology that needs to be understood in pastoral terms. In fact, in a nutshell, what we are saying is that in a church for exiles, the appropriate mode of theological discourse is not historical theology, biblical theology narrowly understood, or systematic theology. It is practical or pastoral theology.

Practical Theology

Practical theology has sometimes struggled to be considered as a genre of theology in its own right. Until relatively recently, practical, applied or pastoral theology meant learning about the skills, competencies and aptitudes that pastors might need in their work with people. It might include counselling on the one hand, or how to conduct a funeral on the other. Nowadays, as the recent *Blackwell Reader in Pastoral and Practical Theology* bears witness, the whole thing has become more sophisticated and complex. It has been defined as: 'a prime place where contemporary experience and the resources of the religious tradition meet in a critical dialogue that is mutually and practically transforming'.[25] I prefer to speak of it, from my perspective, as the point where religious traditions, and particularly biblical traditions, meet and interact with human experiences and situations in such a way that each is potentially open to transformation by the other. What does this mean in practice? It means, on the one hand that I recognize that Christians do not read the Bible as an end in itself; much less because they are interested, in some kind of anthropological way, in the behaviour patterns of ancient civilizations. Christians read the Bible in order to understand the world and God's and their place in it. They read it in a way that will help them interpret their experience. Reading the Bible should mean making a difference to the way we see the world, and that in turn should make a difference to everything else we do as human beings. On the other hand, it means that when I read the Bible, I bring an agenda with me that has been determined by my context. As I read the Bible, I want to find resonances with that context in order to make the kind of connections that might help me to understand better these ancient documents from a distant culture. That in turn may lead to a new understanding of the text. Both text and context interact with each other and both are consequently changed.

Reflection on Text and Experience

Think for a moment of any sermon you have heard or book you have seen or Bible passage you have read which has really changed your view of things, and actually led you to do something you might otherwise not have done. Can you remember the passage now? Read it again, in retrospect, and see if its depth of meaning has changed for you in any way. This is a good exercise to share in a group. If you have never had this experience what is your response to hearing about it? Do you think that this is how Bible reading should be?

The growth of interest in practical theology has coincided with the decline of the dominance of the historical critical method as a means of interpreting biblical texts. In that method, priority was given to the original meaning of the text to its first readers or hearers. If you wanted to discover the truth of a passage you asked a series of questions such as: When was it written, to whom, by whom, in what circumstances? and so on. You might accept that different meanings could attach themselves to texts over time, but always you would ask the same kinds of question about subsequent editions or redactions. These methods were modelled on those used by historians – hence the name – to determine truth objectively, and their adoption owed much to the concerns of Bible scholars to have their work taken seriously by the academic community, during the so-called modern period which lasted from the Enlightenment until a very short time ago. Now more and more scholars are beginning to use methods of studying texts that echo not so much the methods of historians as those of students of literature. The key questions about truth according to this approach are no longer based primarily on what the text said to its original readers. They are based on what it says to us. The reader's context therefore becomes a much more important ingredient in the description of what a text says and means than it used to be. The prime method of reading texts used to be described as *exegesis* – that is a reading out of the text what it contains. Now, increasingly, *eisegesis* is becoming important – that is a reading in to the text from our own context.

This development in the reading of texts and the blossoming of practical theology are both important, I think, for our study. So what are we asserting in saying that practical theology is the appropriate mode of doing theology in a church for exiles? We might consider seven characteristics of practical theology, and see how they relate to, or might give shape to, our enquiry about exile.

1. First, practical theology is dynamic. The aim is not to find the one meaning of a text or the one way of understanding a situation and set them in concrete. If the process of transformation is working as it should, both meanings and understandings should be constantly changing. To this extent some practical theologians have developed ways of describing their work in terms of cycles. Text interacts with context. This leads to changes in the context. The changed context is then brought into new contact with the text. That too is now seen in a new light, and so on. This is a way of doing theology which gives due weight to *process*.

2. It follows from this that practical theology deals with that which is provisional. All theology is for the time being. There are no fixed and final answers. This has effects in terms of the church. There is no one model, no one-size-fits-all paradigm that has to be accommodated regardless of context. Such an approach is ideally suited to a 'for-the-time-being' understanding of church.

3. This has the effect of making practical theology seem

rather messy and disorganized in comparison with other ways of setting about theology. It is not given to systems, order, controls or dogmas. Moreover, it is quite possible that several theologies can be evidenced in just one Christian community because of the different contexts of individual lives. Variety is one aspect of this approach. We have already noted this as a characteristic of the exilic process as well.

4. Practical theology exhibits a particular kind of curiosity. It tries to find ways of reading situations, often relying on the insights of other branches of enquiry such as psychology or sociology. It is courteous towards other disciplines, honours data as important, and is tentative as to its own conclusions. This same style of curiosity is apparent in the texts we have looked at.

5. The theological questions raised within practical theology tend toward that branch of theology traditionally known as ecclesiology. That is, they tend to be the kinds of questions raised for example by Nicholas Bradbury: 'Why keep the church going? Is it really worth it?'.[26] We have seen the close link between the Old Testament texts and the identity of the faith community; and between the New Testament texts and ecclesiology.

6. As you would expect then, practical theology will have a particular interest in the pragmatic rather then the theoretical. Why bother with the church? would be seen as an urgent and serious question, to which a practical response is required. That does not mean that God has to be restricted to the terms of what we can practically imagine. It does mean that we take seriously a God who acts, who was incarnate, and who enlivens the church still by his Spirit. But practical theology does ask the further question: So what does this amount to in practice? This is very much the approach we saw in the Pauline letters.

7. The characteristic activity associated with practical

theology is *reflection*. The theologian is constantly being asked to facilitate the interactions referred to above, and that process is called theological reflection. Again, different authors have devised ways of doing this. Most of them are common sense to those for whom the whole enterprise is coherent in the first place. We have described the birth and growth of both Old and New Testaments in terms of their being theological reflections.

On the face of it, then, this is a way of approaching theology that seems made for situations of temporary settledness. Brueggemann's approach is well-fitted to practical theology though he himself does not use the term. He is well aware of the cultural demands of the post-modern era and suspicious of any suggestion of 'a given reality'. His instinct is that the most appropriate way to apply exilic theology is through preaching. A way of understanding theology that was itself so bound up with articulated responses to practical crises lends itself, as we have seen in the book of Job, to dialogue as a means of expression, and in *Cadences of Home* Brueggemann sets out what he hears as the voices from exile to which reply must be made.[27]

In Chapter 2 I spoke of the response to exile in the texts as a 'theological reflection'. I identified a *style* which accompanies this reflection. 'On the one hand it is creative, exploratory and almost mischievously innovative. But on the other it is tentative, humble, accepting the provisionality and unresolvedness of the issues with which it deals.' In Chapter 3 we saw that the book of Job 'represents something of a triumph for unresolvedness over against resolution: for possibility over against definition: for process over against system'. Both of these conclusions correspond easily with the assumptions of practical theology.

The book of Job is a cry against theories and systems, and we might argue that that same suspicion is mirrored in the move towards definite institutions and marks of identity in the P tradition. This tradition has a way of doing theology which leads in ecclesiological directions. How will the community be identified? What is it for? What will its ministry look like? What will its worship achieve? From the New Testament context this is also a prime concern of 1 Peter with its distinctive ecclesiological thinking and its reflections on worship. Of course one could describe both of these in institutional terms that would be anathema to Job. His demand above all is for a theology that takes his context seriously and is not so institutional as to be inflexible to the point of uselessness. This pragmatic imperative is one we have identified in practical theology. Another lesson to be learned from Job is that these questions matter, and that dealing with them is urgent to enable meaningful life to continue. Urgency is almost a defining characteristic of practical theology.

Conclusion

What then is the most appropriate contemporary application of the exilic process, and what does it have to tell us about the possible shape of church life in our times? My first conclusion is that the exilic process shows practical theology at work. It derives from a practical situation of significance to which an urgent response of theological reflection is required because fundamental questions are raised by the experience. It understands the need for that context to be taken seriously and the consequent reflection leads to the rewriting of traditions as well as to some completely fresh understandings which need to be applied to new contexts, if only in the experimental form of stories and novels. Its most appropriate application today is to situations in which individuals and communities demand similar serious and urgent reflection. In some parts of the world that may mean that exilic theology is appropriate for a whole church, and that it may help it to understand its identity and vocation better. In western culture it is less likely that the church can realistically see itself as in exile, and there are real dangers in 'pretending' to be in exile and adopting the tone of a suffering community when in fact it is not suffering at all.

Churches that do that will not only perceive themselves as being in a hostile or indifferent community. They may discover that to maintain their identity they have to develop a quite artificial and uncalled for hostility to their environment which will drive them in a sectarian direction. Churches like that run the danger of losing vital lines of communication between themselves and reality. There is something quite psychologically odd about living life as if elsewhere, which is ultimately unsustainable, particularly for those members whose lives are lived wholly or mostly in the real world, and who have to acknowledge it as such. A church thus understood has very little mission potential. It is notable in 1 Peter for example that the only forms of mission activity one could point to are 'service' and 'example'. This may have real power in a situation of actual suffering, but in a situation where we are using the language but not actually suffering at all, it is doubtful that they would. Much more likely is that this church would become very inward-looking, concentrating on its own rules and constitution, trying to contain the anxieties it generated and finally looking more like a ghetto than a colony. And what's more, for churches like this there is no way back. There is nothing the world can do to persuade them. They are like Jonah, sulking because God has repented against Nineveh.

However, although it is illegitimate to define the church in a way that for ever sets it at odds with the world in which it is placed, it is still true that the church must exhibit restlessness. The exilic community remains aware of the provisionality of conclusions; the new sense of the grandeur and unimagined possibility of God; the unresolved nature of questions about justice and forgiveness; and the evidence that the problem of evil has not finally been solved. Within this wider context of restlessness the church finds a temporary home. And this home must be regarded as home in the fullest sense. Jeremiah's remarkable message to the first exiles is salutary.

> Build houses and live in them; plant gardens and eat what they produce. Take wives and have sons and daughters; take wives for your sons, and give your daughters in marriage, that they may bear sons and daughters; multiply there and do not decrease. But seek the welfare of the city where I have sent you into exile, and pray to the Lord on its behalf, for in its welfare you will find your welfare. (Jeremiah 29:5–7)

And so it turns out that exiles are more like pilgrims than tourists. They want and need to be part of a community which is involved with its context and which expects to be changed by it. This is how the exilic process can find application. The church is a church for exiles. It is home for them, and as an institution it is at home in its context . . . for the time being.

6

Voices from Exile

Introduction

In the days when I used to make and present religious television programmes I remember doing an item on teenage
suicide. As a result of doing that item I became aware of an
organization called 'Voices from Care', which was a group
of young people who had all had horrendous experiences
whilst in local authority homes. There was something
about that simple title which has stuck with me. Trying to
understand any human phenomenon becomes so much
more real when we hear the voices of those who experienced it. That is all the more true when the experience is
one of suffering, and our access to it appears closed. To
hear the voices from that experience confers a sense both of
privilege and of authenticity. Some scholars claim that we
can hear voices from the Exile that clearly.

Reflection on Experience

Can you think of any time when you have been able
to gain special insight into a situation by listening to
the voices, the testimony, of those who have been
involved directly? Perhaps you have been able to
speak to a refugee from war, or someone who has
been personally affected by something you would

only otherwise have heard about at second hand. What difference is there between hearing something directly like this and reading about it in a news-paper? Is it any better to see it on the TV? What kind of witness do you think we can expect to find in the Bible? Does thinking about these questions affect the way you approach the text?

Voices from the First Exile and Their Interpretation

If practical theology is to be the dominant theme of a modern exilic community called the church, in its tempo-rary permanence, its settled restlessness, then we shall need to listen carefully to the voices that come from *its* exiles, and to have that same sense of hearing something sig-nificant. We might then be in a position to meet them with resources from the traditions. This is a method which Brueggemann adopts in his *Cadences of Home*. Referring to the initial Exile he identifies six 'circumstances of exile' which he proposes to 'interface' with scriptural resources.[28] I have already referred to these circumstances but they are worth repeating. He believes that exiles:

- Grieve and resent the loss of what will never again be;
- Have an experience of being orphaned;
- Know the power of despair;
- Experience what he calls the 'profaned absence' of God;
- Live with new moral questions about fault and blame;
- Have a preoccupation with self.

Since his aim is to outline how one might preach to exiles today, the next stage of his process is to apply each of these 'circumstances' to a current experience relating to the church he knows. He believes that the church should offer an alternative assertion of reality to that of the world. In his experience church members experience the world 'out there' as 'a jungle', in comparison with which the church is a 'zone of freedom'. This is a place where truths can be declared against the odds. The truths he identifies are mostly about the 'dominant culture'. They are related to the scriptural resources outlined.

The context in which he preaches is therefore defined by the kinds of voices that say:

- That our sense of loss and sadness is serious and honourable, and one need not prop up or engage in denial.
- That our rootedness enables us to belong so that we are not swept away by every wind of doctrine, every market seduction, or every economic coercion, knowing who we are.
- That the promises of the creator surge in our life and in our world, so that the manipulable despair of the hopeless, which turns folk into commodity consumers, is not the live edge of our existence.
- That there is a holy, awesome presence that persists against the emptied profanation of promiscuous economic and lustful sexuality, that true desire is for the presence that overrides all of our trivialized desires that are now robbed of authority.
- That the world is not morally coherent, but there is a deep incongruity in which we live, that we need neither to resolve, explain or deny. A raw, ragged openness is linked to the awesome reality of God's holiness.
- That we are always about to be domesticated; we have these narrative models of resistance, defiance and negotiation that remind us there is more to life than conformist obedience or shameful accommodation. We know the names of those who have faced with freedom the trouble that is caused by faith [the novels which name heroes: Joseph, Esther and Daniel].[29]

This is the way he applies the exilic process and this is what he believes it has to say to his church where he lives, and as he understands it. He outlines the biblical resources at each point that address these voices from exile.

Reflection on Experience

Read through the list above again. Is there anything at all that you recognize here? Are these voices that you also hear, or do you think they belong to a different situation? In the following sections I shall set out some of the voices from exile which I hear, and to which I believe the church must respond. As you read through them do you recognize these voices? What do you hear in your own situation which you think should be added to this list. Should anything be taken away?

It is not for us to judge the success with which he has read his own context, but Brueggemann does set out a model, which could be called a practical theological model, for dealing with both text and context. It forces us to ask, are there other different voices from exile which we need to hear, and for which we might try to find biblical resources for dialogue?

Voices from Today's Exiles

The place where most pastors might hear such voices from exile will be in connection with tragic bereavement. There is something universal about the cry of the suffering. Unusual death, the death of a child or a young spouse presents people from within western culture with formidable challenges. The most frequent initial responses to these events are anger and guilt. One is also often struck, as a pastor, by the vulnerability that the bereaved display. This is a time for priestly assurances of forgiveness, and pastoral displays of quiet gentleness. But before long there will be attempts to make sense of what has happened in a way that will make life bearable in the future. Some narrative will be conceived to 'explain' what has happened, for the benefit of other young members of the family perhaps. Symbols will be sought to mark the significance of this time and its events. Flowers, candles, cards, domestic rituals will all be brought into play. A funeral liturgy has to be arranged with hymns, readings, prayers which will be expected to give a framework of coherence. At heart the cry here is: Let there be meaning! The truly unbearable thing would be that this death should represent a purposeless, meaningless waste, and be seen as an admission that there is no point in believing or behaving in particular ways. So a great deal is at stake. The question: How could God let this happen? is a serious question which hopes for an answer in terms of: God lets this happen because . . . and unfortunately all too often that is what pastors provide. Then the next reflective stage sees the inadequacy of any answer framed in those terms, and feels spiritually betrayed. Here is a cry from exile, requiring a theological response; and today's pastors have to do rather more than Job's friends to provide it.

If those whose framework of meaning is shattered, mirror one kind of Old Testament Exile experience, another group whose voice we should hear are those who have a vocational stake in the pre-exile understanding of things. I have in mind those who have based their lives' work on assumptions about God which seem now to be rendered redundant by new experiences. There is something quite pathetic about real redundancy. The area in which I have worked pastorally for most of my life has given me ample opportunity to observe it. I used to work in a parish where most of the men worked in coalmines, while their wives worked in a factory that made clockwork clocks. Those who didn't work in coal, worked in steel. Within just a few years all these jobs had gone. The world had moved on. The saddest thing is when, for individuals, their work really was considered to be a vocation. It was, they believed, what they were called to do, and so one of the landmarks of their life. It made them who they were. In like fashion there are those who have a vocational stake in a particular understanding of how God works in the world, and for them, experiences which seem to point to redundancy are hugely significant. I refer here not only to disillusioned clergy to whom I have spoken and who feel that their whole life has been wasted, but to others who have worked sacrificially in caring or volunteer capacities; those who have given up much to work for justice and now wonder if they have really achieved anything and whether it was all worth it. And particularly I refer to those who have done so not because of any political agenda but simply because they believed that it was what God willed, and despite all the disappointments and set-backs that belief kept them going. The Old Testament people were chosen and elect. The cry of the vocationally redundant today is an equivalent cry from exile.

The Old Testament people were also people of a Covenant. As we see the Covenant idea expressed in the writings of the prophets of the eighth century BCE such as Amos, Micah and Hosea, we realize how the Covenant is more than a set of rules. It is an understanding that relationship lies at the heart of meaning in life, and that loving, graceful relationships are the way in which life is lived most abundantly. Today, too, particularly in the West, there is debate about the most appropriate way of relating one to another. At one level this is tied up with questions about power and its abuse. At another it is connected to the debate about the future of marriage, and how much sense it makes in comparison with, say, serial monogamy. You only have to attend a religious wedding ceremony to realize afresh how much is at stake for those who have risked everything on a covenant approach to life. Alternatively, you only have to speak to the faithful spouse of an adulterous partner to realize what has been lost. Those who really believe that faithful, sacrificial, sacramental relationships offer the key to meaning in life often have a hard time of it. Serious living often seems to compare badly with superficial living. The assurance that such modern covenant people look for, represents another cry from exile. That is the cry which wants to know that the Covenant is still valid.

The Old Testament people of God worked out who they were in relation to God. God was part of their system of establishing identity. The Exile posed new questions about who they really were – if anyone. Today, many people experience crises of identity but there is a particular group of people whose cry we need to hear and that is those for whom God was, if you like, a last resort in conferring identity. As Lamentations 3:24 puts it: 'The Lord is all I've got, therefore I will hope in him.' There are people who are so unloved, so disregarded, so dehumanized by the world in which they live that their only hope of esteem or worth comes from their sense of being loved by God. We might think of seriously handicapped people; people who have no ability to communicate; people whose lifestyle is at odds with the majority as gay or lesbians; people who are lonely through their inability to make relationships; drug users; those who have committed some grave offence against society, and so on. If God goes, what happens to them?

And of course we must add to these voices all those others who have discovered in some other way the bankruptcy of the old system. Included amongst them will be those who have become disillusioned because of the church itself. How can the church shield its own reputation at the cost of an abused child? How can the church preach one thing and be seen blatantly to be doing another? There will be those who have discovered in a thousand ways that life is not fair, that people do not get what they deserve and that religion is no guarantee of success. There will be those who have never known religious life, but whilst we are thinking of exiles we must have special concern for those who have become disillusioned by what they believed it would offer, and what it then failed to offer. Two people pray for sick relatives. Both die and the neighbour's relative gets better – and she never goes near church and is a well-known ne'er-do-well.

Then there are the cries of those who have unresolved forgiveness issues, and who need to believe that resolution is possible if life is to be coped with in the future. How often, as a pastor, have I heard the words, 'I just can't forgive him', knowing that what is really required is an assurance that ultimately forgiveness is possible in life. Issues around divorce and unfaithfulness in marriage are, in my experience, among the things people find most difficulty with in this connection. Other family disputes are also high on the list. A society that values victims and even seeks to persuade those who have been affected by unfortunate accidents, that they are indeed victims and deserve satisfaction from someone, makes it all the more difficult to live with unresolved forgiveness issues.

Bible Links

All of these are examples suggested by Old Testament Exile parallels. But we see the same issues rehearsed, the same issues at stake in the theological responses of Paul and 1 Peter. Here too, especially, are issues about *undeserved suffering*. These were particularly acute in the early church, and their being seen as an obstacle to belief may well have occasioned the writing of the First Gospel. How can Jesus be God and suffer? How can Jesus be God and die? It is Paul who has the most thoroughly worked through theology of *vocation* in the New Testament, related to sharing in Christ's sufferings and showing the importance of responding to that cry. The questions about *love and covenant* are also current as we see in the united response of the New Testament, as was the issue of *belonging to God and being known by him*. The *resolution of forgiveness* could be said to be the New Testament's basic theme. In other words these exile cries, as we have called them, were not simply the cries of a bygone age, nor peculiar to our own. They were the cries to which the post-exilic religious community had to make response, but they also set the agenda for the New Testament exile theologians. They are universal questions, and the church's life today needs to be informed by them.

These cries need what Brueggemann might call 'a new construal of reality', that is, they need new theology, or at least, theology which is prepared to look at new and risky areas. They need coping mechanisms for life that are realistic. They need statements of identity that will help people to have a sense of belonging and give some meaning to community. They need some vocational rationale for their life's work and a means of living together that enables them to do just that, without constant anxiety, guilt and dis-ease. And this is not just an internal reordering as far as the church is concerned. This is not just a rescue attempt for those who were once members and have left. This is actually part of the church's mission; because the questions we have identified, the cries we have heard, are universal questions and cries; and all who want to take life seriously (and at some time that means all of us) will ask and cry them. It is not perhaps claiming too much to say that the dialogue this will involve is a large part of what the church is for, if not all it is for. That is how it was conceived post-Exile, and it could be argued that that is how it was seen post-crucifixion as well. The church is the place where the fundamental questions raised by the possibilities of God's absence can dialogue with the traditions that assert his presence.

Churches as Theological Communities

But how can the church enable the dialogue to happen? How can the church be the church in this sense? What is required here is that churches become overtly much more *theological*. Churches cannot continue without theology. It is their life blood. Far too many things happen in churches by accident, without thought, carelessly. Symbols and liturgies are introduced without real thought to their context or what they might communicate. Programmes are embarked upon, based on other people's ideas, for all the wrong reasons to do with church numerical growth for those who desperately want or need to see results. Far too seldom is the question asked: Why bother at all? Attending many church services one does not have the sense that here is a community that considers what the occasion says as fundamentally significant (and indeed some of the ones that do, frighten the pants off you because of how they view its significance). Church life is too often characterized by a culture of carelessness and thoughtlessness in which it is difficult to deal in any way with questions of fundamental significance.

What we might provide here are some theological pointers, based on the texts we have looked at, towards the style and culture of a theological church, a church which has just discovered the need for new theological creativity, which has just discovered its need to articulate its activity afresh, in the way that the exile churches of Old and New Testaments did – what Brueggemann describes as telling the stories that declared who they were. We might begin with the story of D.

Theological Terrorists?

I'm never quite sure how loudly to applaud the activities and achievements of those we have simply called 'D'. Were they fundamentalist fanatics or visionary innovators? They were the young radicals who with the co-operation of King Josiah, managed essentially to reinvent the religion of Yahweh in the face of the threat of Exile which they saw more clearly than anyone, informed as they probably were by prophets of the eighth century, whose words they may have been responsible for preserving. We have some insight into the extent of their hopes and expectations through the disappointment of Jeremiah, one of their number. We see their manifesto in the book of Deuteronomy and their telling of the story of Israel in the books from Joshua through to 2 Kings, generally known as the Deuteronomistic history or D history. The practical effect of their reforms was first to close down all the shrines and religious sites of worship out in the sticks. These were administered by priests over whom there were no 'quality control' checks, and who apparently had no common understanding of what Yahweh religion was about. We see from books like Amos that religion delivered in this way was largely disregarded anyway. People kept the religious calendar but without any real sense that this was important for anything other than cultural or nostalgic reasons. There was an impatience to get back to the real business of (commercial) life. Religion and morality were seen as quite unconnected and the nation had no sense of anything being at stake in terms of its religious life. Religious privileges were themselves abused. The D response to this was to centralize worship at (probably) one shrine, which enabled control and oversight and guaranteed one centre of excellence.

Reflection on Text

You might like to take this opportunity to have a look
through some of the portions of one of the eighth-
century prophets which detail the case against
Israel, and to which the D writers were responding.
Amos is probably a good place to start. You might
reflect on **2:6–8, 4:1, 4–6, 5:12f., 21–24, 6:4–7, 8:4–6**.
This picture is, of course, presented by those of D's
outlook. Does reading these passages help you to
understand them better, and give a clearer view of
what life was like in those times? Can you see any
connections between that situation and your own?

Worship was particularly important for these people. It
was a means of recital, of telling the story which maintained the identity of the people, and which reminded them
who they were, what they were called to, and what their
covenant responsibilities were. It was also a means of
conveying religious teaching from one generation to another.
It can also be seen as a perceptive response to the religious
needs of the people, to organize their spirituality with new
and meaningful symbols and to make sure everyone got
something out of it. The command to rejoice is a constant
refrain in Deuteronomy (for example 12:12, 14:26, 16:14).
From now on, a large part of religious observance was
going to be transferred from the sacred building to the
home – just one of the ways in which this group sought to
break down barriers between the sacred and the secular.
The Passover would be celebrated within the context of
a family meal with story-telling at its heart, religious
education would take place in the home and religion would
become a matter of everyday discourse, symbolized through
everyday things. It would become the natural mode of
Israel's existence. We know about this movement through

the words of those who were enthusiastic about it, so it is not easy to assess how it was experienced by its opponents, whether as benign or as the work of some Taleban-like group of fanatics. Certainly they employed fantastically aggressive language as they described the right of Israel to the land (see for example Deuteronomy 20:16–18). But they also displayed very modern and one could almost say, liberal, interpretations of how society should be organized (see for example the understanding displayed towards potential soldiers 20:1–9). The writings were calculated to give a new sense of identity and worth to a people who had lost their way. 'You are the children of the Lord your God. You are a people holy to the Lord your God; it is you the Lord has chosen out of all the peoples of the earth to be his people, his treasured possession' (14:1a, 2). This is not the place to embark upon a full critique of these writings, but we might note for our purposes possible similarities between the situation addressed by these activists and our own.

In our society there is no copyright on the word 'Christian'. Any group of people can describe themselves in that way and so bring the whole into disrepute. There is little control over the use of the word 'church', though the law does demand that some concept of prayer accompany such claims. The proliferation of so-called Christian groups means in practice that the term has become almost meaningless, and certainly quite confusing to non-Christians. Even within what we in the mainstream like to call the mainstream, that is, the historic churches, there are fundamental disagreements about what it means to be Christian, such that alliances often form across denominations between those of like mind. Within a particular denomination disputes can be bitter. It even proved possible for some minority dissident groups within Anglicanism to question whether the present Archbishop of Canterbury was Christian, before his appointment. In society generally

Christianity is thought to be peripheral to real life. Worship is often experienced as quite unconnected with its context and conducted as if nothing significant is happening. For the D writers these were among the reasons why the Exile happened, and are a kind of response to its having happened of the told-you-so variety. But they also function as a description of how things must change, and the direction religious life must take when the land is re-entered, post-Exile. In other words they are a reflection on what the religious life consists of for Israel in the new times. That also provides pointers for us.

We see in these writers the combination of statement with story. We see also the recognition that a strong statement of identity is required as part of the story. That is, the story needs to declare who we are. Everything else about religious life stems from that. They say: 'We are treasured by God. The land is our evidence. Now choose whether the disaster is to happen again or whether you've learned your lesson.' The importance of breaking the division between the sacred and the secular, and the making 'natural' of religious discourse, rather than its just being a technical language used by experts on specific occasions, is also notable. The movement of religion to the home has been largely responsible for its survival in Judaism, and is a necessity for diaspora groups of other kinds. Ironically, the Christian religion began in homes and has moved in the opposite direction. Most fundamentally of all, the D writers are not prepared to continue as if religion doesn't matter. They believe it matters greatly for the state, and for the welfare (*shalom*) of the people, and as something that matters deeply it cannot be allowed to drift. The Exile is evidence of what happens when it does. John Lennon might imagine a world with no religion, optimistically, as one with no wars either, but the D writers see a world with no religion as dangerous and pointless. What this tells us is that religious life in our post-exilic world needs to have a

theological style which treats religious confession more
seriously; is prepared to be daringly innovative and ruth-
lessly unsentimental in regard to dead wood; which connects
with people authentically, and treats worship particularly
carefully as a characteristic expression of both religious
tradition and human agenda. That is the place above all
where practical theology is done.

Learning from P

From the P tradition we can take different lessons. These
writers also told the story of Israel in the books 1 and 2
Chronicles, Ezra and Nehemiah, but they did not have just
one book, like Deuteronomy, in which to set out their
manifesto. Instead we are made aware of that by their
particular contribution to the Pentateuch. These writers,
like the D writers, recognize the importance of the question
of sin for the community. The D writers are responding to
the question: How could God let the Exile happen? and so
one might expect them to take a more pessimistic view of
history. The P writers are responding to the question: How
can the religious community survive and continue in the
future? so you might expect their response to be more up-
beat. The D writers, who find common cause here with the
older J traditions of the Pentateuch, write their history of
humankind as if it were 'a history of sin'.[30] The J traditions
begin with the story of the Fall (Genesis 2, 3), and the D
tradition also begins with an account of original sin
(Deuteronomy 1:6–8, 19–46). The P writers take a kinder
view. In P there is no Fall, no Cain and Abel, no golden calf.
The tower of Babel story in Genesis 11 is subverted in its
conclusion that scattering the people was a punishment.
The P tradition describes it as a blessing (Genesis 10:32).

Reflection on Text

It is actually worth taking the trouble to compare **Genesis 11:1-9** and **Genesis 10**. Both seek to describe why there are many nations and languages spread over a wide area, with examples of national difference and particularity. Which do you find the most appealing? Is national difference and language difference a blessing or a curse, do you think? What kind of experience, do you think, made the P account different from the original?

The P account of original sin is at Genesis 6 where the sin is described as violence (6:11). Walking with God, as did Noah, means avoiding violence. P has two other examples of original sin. One is the rejection of the gift of the land (Numbers 13:32, 14:36f.) and the other is the failure of Israel's leaders to trust Yahweh (Numbers 20:1-13). All of these are mature reflections on the debate about sin.

The P writers also contributed to the debate about Covenant. For them the Covenant was God's gift. It was everlasting and could not be undone. As Klein puts it: 'P solved the problem of broken covenant by restricting the term covenant to those unilateral promises made to Noah and Abraham and by giving Sinai a different meaning for Israel's faith.'[31] The rainbow will show that God has not forgotten, and is a symbol of the permanence of the agreement. God has not forgotten in other ways too. It is the P writers who are responsible for the recurring 'God remembered'. (Genesis 8:1, Exodus 2:24, 6:5). The theological problem they perceive is that of finding assurances for people who believe that God has either withdrawn or forgotten. P's solution is to tell the story in a way that shows people in the past have felt like this as well but God will remember as he always did. The promise of fertility made in Genesis, chapters 1, 9, 17 and 35 is actually brought to a climax in a land outside Israel, in Egypt of all places, in exile (Exodus 1:7). Allied to this is a theology one could call sacramental, which allows God's presence to be perceived by the faithful in ways other than 'showing results'. Genesis 1 is a kind of liturgy, which opens up the possibility of God's being known throughout his creation. This is supported by a new and comprehensive institutional form of worship and religion whose purpose is to make real the abiding of God with his people, as well as to provide definitive marks of identity such as Sabbath observance and male circumcision.

P's theology is not aggressive or driven. There is a degree of gentleness and tentativeness which marks it out from the D writings. As a school associated with the rise of creation theology there is a sense of awe and wonder at the newly discovered greatness of God as well as a kind of humility that shows honest acceptance of what we don't know. This is theology after experience. The idea of a healing God is introduced in a new way, God is described as Israel's physician at Exodus 15:26, and at least one scholar thinks that the health of the nation after testing becomes a mark of God's relationship in a way that will reach a climax only in the healing miracles of Jesus.[32]

It is this style of humility and tentativeness with regard to what we assert about God which we might note for these new times. The important thing is to trust in a God for whom there is no specific evidence outside the eyes of faith. We see then the importance of worship, and of sacramental forms which assert that God is near or present despite his holy awesomeness. It is in response to this holiness that human activity and behaviour takes its cue, as in the so-called Holiness Code of Leviticus 17 – 26. The problems that the writers deal with are comparable with those of the D writings: sin, God's perceived indifference, identity, what is the point of religion, what is the link between belief and behaviour, and so on. The responses are different but they do show that each of these schools is aware of its context and concerned to respond to it. The main difference is in the shape of the new community envisaged. The D community has a very different understanding of the religious life from that of P, which is far more institutional and sacerdotal. This P style is reflected in the writings of the prophet Ezekiel who couches his vision of what needs to change and what it will look like when it has (that is, his eschatological vision) in terms of a brand new temple. Interestingly this is precisely the idiom chosen to describe the church in the New Testament exilic 1 Peter, which also has suffering as a theme.

Other Old Testament Pointers

It is not only in the telling of these stories that the Old Testament people respond with literary creativity. From the exilic portions of Isaiah we see that forgiveness and suffering are once again regarded as important on that agenda. It is here that the idea of redemptive suffering finds its highest Old Testament expression, in the person of the suffering servant. What we might learn from this projection, as from the 'novels' as we have called them, and especially Job, is the importance of finding vehicles of communication which will enable people to engage fully with new ideas. Whatever else they are, the songs of the suffering servant are arresting pieces of communication, their popularity evidenced by their use in later traditions. They might also give us clues as to where sightings of God might be found, a crucial question for these new times when the old certainties no longer hold.

Reflection on Text

Look again at a portion of text you first considered in Chapter 3, namely **Isaiah 52:13—53:15**. This is one of the servant songs. What is it about this description of the servant which makes it so compelling, do you think? What clues do you think it gives us for new sightings of God?

They encourage us to look again at what it might mean to declare God is present in worship, or the religious establishment; they encourage us to find new assertions about God (God was in Babylon); but they also encourage us to push out the boundaries towards where the fundamental questions are being asked. So they urge us to look for new sightings, and to find new ways of communicating them in a way that those with the questions can understand.

The books of Ruth and Jonah, as well as the creation theology expounded in Isaiah and P remind us of the ecumenical nature of the theological enterprise. The apocalyptic writings give us a further dimension with regard to human history. The ecumenical style is one which is well-aware of the inbuilt resistance to anything unknown or foreign. It is therefore quite aggressive and accusing, asking its opponents to put up or shut up (see for example Isaiah 45:20-25, 46). It declares things beyond our imaginations but inspires us with a vision of what must change, and with that we can identify.

We see this style and agenda replayed to some extent in the New Testament exile writings. Once again sin and suffering are key concerns. The writings of Paul and 1 Peter make it possible to speak easily and naturally about suffering and death rather than to make them taboo. They go much further than does the Old Testament in redescribing God, but you would expect that because they've just had a new and definitive sighting of God in Jesus. But it is precisely that sighting which has precipitated the crisis. Now there has to be new talk about weakness and vulnerability among the sentiments of hope for vindication. Vindication itself has to be rethought.

A Theological Church

So what have we learned about the style and culture of a more overtly theological church?

- First and foremost, it will be a church that has a sense of *the significance of being a church*. It will understand that fundamental questions of meaning and purpose, the things that make life bearable or unbearable for people, are routinely dealt with here; that the cries of the exiles are heard; that commentary on the issues of the day is offered here on the basis that it matters; that the traditions about God, and the sightings to date are honoured.
- It will also mean that these *traditions are seen as part of a living process* in which it is impossible to constrain God, and whose interpretation may vary according to the context of the hearers.
- It will have a *robust* attitude to tradition, enabling it to jettison bankrupt models and modes of church life. It will have an *adventurous* attitude towards funding new models and modes of church life. It will have a *humility* towards what can be asserted as well as a *gentleness* towards those who are raw with questions.
- It will see *the importance of worship* as a characteristic and defining activity, and will accept the need to find ways of asserting God's presence and of asserting the particular identity of the religious community, in worship.
- It will want to *relate its local concerns to a much wider canvas*, raising questions about human destiny and that

of the world. It will want to find ways of bearing witness to the God of all history, creation and peoples with vision and imagination.

In addition to all of these it will need to have a way of being a *textual community*. It was the Exile, I have argued, which led to the writing of the Old Testament. It was the crisis of the crucifixion which led essentially to the writing of the New Testament. Exilic churches are characterized above all by their need to make and communicate theology.

7

Textual Communities:
Theologians at Work

Introduction

I have often displayed a not very commendable reticence
when asked on holiday what I do for a living. This is partly
born of the experience of discovering that so many of my
chosen holiday retreats appear to have been taken over for
the week by Sunday School teachers, church choristers and
the recently bereaved. But it also bears witness to an awareness that to describe my work using either the terms
'church' or 'theologian' will probably mean that for the rest
of the vacation I shall be marked out as someone whose
relation to the rest of the human race is peripheral at best. I
recognize then that it is taking a risk to advocate the view
that in order for the church to grasp the opportunities of its
exilic inheritance it needs to have a stronger sense of the
significance of being a church and to be theologically
creative. I wonder what picture springs to mind when we
hear a description of the church as a textual or theological
community. Perhaps we imagine something very scholarly,
bookish and earnest; something rather remote from the
ordinary business of life and accessible only to experts.
Nothing could be further from the intention. Following the
lead of the D writers in the Old Testament, the aim of such
communities would actually be to bring theology out of the

closet and out of the control of those who now, all too often, seem to have it without either enthusiasm or inspiration. It would be to make the activities of theological reflection available to all, and to encourage everyone to accept that they are potential theologians, among their other vocations.

Reflection on Experience

What does the term 'theologian' mean to you? Which of the following words might seem appropriate: boring, clever, academic, exciting, stimulating, adventurous? Could you imagine yourself being one? Would you want to be! Now think of anything which makes religious or church life exciting and interesting for you. What part does *theology* play in producing that? Does thinking along these lines change your view at all? You might like to save your reflections to compare them with your views at the end of the chapter.

Theological Communities

Like D, such a view of the religious community aims to bring it closer to everyday life, linked to experience and conversation, a seven-day thing. It hopes to produce a new understanding of what church is for, which is recognizably urgent and relevant, and which will lead to a new confidence in being part of it and a new sense of enjoyment in that participation. And that, in turn, leads to a new impetus for mission. One of the (usually unspoken) barriers to mission activity is that people can't think of a reason why anyone else should want to join. There's no clear idea of 'what's in it for them'. A theological community has a clear idea of what it is for, and an expectation that it will appeal to all those who want to engage fully in life. Like the D communities this life is reflected in a new and innovative immediacy to worship. This is a form of church life that everyone can get excited about, everyone can have a stake in and everyone get something out of. Such communities are not textual in the sense that they're always reading books. They are textual in the sense of their awareness that they are creating new theology.

Some people may say that churches should be made up of disciples, not theologians. The two are not mutually exclusive. These theologians are disciples in two ways. First, questions of vocation – what people are called to be and do – will constantly be revisited. Not only will this be one of the main reasons for such reflection, but it should be one of the main areas where that theological reflection will produce results. Second, members of this kind of church will be disciples in the sense that, like the communities envisaged by P, they will trust in God without looking for, and testing God by, results. Their faith will be a relationship thing, not an analytical, cerebral, academic, matter of judgement. These will be the post-exile people who trust rather than fear. They will not be the western, post-Enlightenment people who believe rather than doubt. After all, the first Christian theologians, those responsible for writing the New Testament, and those who informed them, were themselves disciples. Some may say that this view leaves no spiritual space, downgrades worship and dismisses activities like prayer. On the contrary: worship is crucial in such communities (see Chapter 8), but has a particular definition. What I have described as theological reflection is close to what many people understand by prayer anyway. Looking at the world in which we live through the eyes of a spiritual tradition, and allowing that dialogue to 'happen', is an experience that many mystics and spiritual leaders would recognize. Textual communities aim to make this an experience open to all.

New Testament Theological Communities

What I see as new and refreshing in the New Testament is that people felt that they had permission to be theologically creative. They were no longer inhibited by authority structures and hierarchies. Like the temple curtain, those kinds of restrictive barrier had been broken. Probably the most important discovery in Gospel study over the last thirty or so years of the twentieth century has been the thesis that the Gospel writers were creative theologians in their own right. When Gospel study began, Matthew, Mark, Luke and John were thought of as observers and recorders. At a later stage of scholarship when there was more reticence about the exact identity of the authors, they were thought to be dispassionate collectors of traditions. But towards the end of the twentieth century they were recognized as people with an argument to win and a people to influence. Not only did they choose traditions carefully and selectively but they combined and presented them in a singular way, designed perhaps for a specific community in a particular place at a particular time in particular circumstances. Scholars became interested in the make up of these communities, and in questions as to why a particular way of addressing them had been chosen.

Reflection on Text

If you want to join in this kind of activity you might read **Luke 13:1–9**. This passage only occurs in Luke. We don't find it in Matthew, Mark or John. It comes in a section where fundamental questions are being placed in the mouths of those whom Jesus meets on his way to crucifixion in Jerusalem, which is itself suggestive. This particular passage mentions two events which commentators agree must have been well-known and contemporary, the stuff of general conversation. Both raise questions about undeserved and scandalous suffering and their relationship with sin – the very stuff of the exilic tradition. On the one hand some people have been the subject of political killings whilst participating in a religious act. On the other there has been a terrible accident. The Siloam 18 had been killed as a tower collapsed on top of them. Imagine how tabloid papers would treat both incidents today and the kind of 'unanswerable' questions they would pose for religion. Now see how Luke addresses those questions and tells a new story to illustrate his point. These things had happened in Jerusalem and this was an issue for his community which other writers did not have to address in the same way.

There are still many questions unanswered about the process of Gospel formation. For me, some of the most interesting are about the relationship between the Gospel writer as *the theologian*, and the community. How was this person chosen, or was he self-selected, recognizing a vocation? How did he relate to the rest of the community? Was he like the poet-in-residence now popular in schools and other institutions? Was he seen to have a distinctive ministry? The term 'evangelist' only occurs in the New Testament three times. The most illuminating is probably Ephesians 4:11f. where the author (probably someone writing in the tradition of Paul but after his time) is listing the gifts of ministry. 'Evangelist' is one of these ministries whose aim is in turn 'to equip the saints for the work of ministry, for building up the Body of Christ'. That suggests to me a close relationship between theologian and community and a relationship based on the understanding that the role of the theologian is to enable the community to participate more fully in the theological task. Certainly this hands-on understanding of the job seems a long way from the book-and-study-bound picture of evangelists we sometimes have. Of the other two occurrences of the word in the New Testament, one is at 2 Timothy 4:5, again relatively late, where it acts as a more general description of the work to which Timothy is called. The other is Acts 21:8 where we hear of Philip the Evangelist. We already know that Philip was a deacon, indeed the passage reasserts that he was one of the seven (Acts 6:5). We also get an insight into the variety of his ministry in chapter 8. It may be that he is called an evangelist here simply to distinguish him from Philip the Apostle. But it may also be, as Larkin (1995) believes, that 'our modern appropriation of the term may be too specialised', noting that, 'evangelists must aim for pioneer crosscultural church planting, the missionary work of apostles'.[33]

As we think of what modern textual or theological communities might be like, I believe we need to think imaginatively about these early communities exulting in their new freedom to articulate new discoveries about God in a new vernacular. We need to see them as people like us, looking for those who have both the skills and the calling to equip us to participate in the theological task ourselves. It is in that way that we shall have both the interest and the understanding to believe that Christian life is worthwhile.

Reflection on Experience

What do you think is the place of 'experts' in the church? What should they be experts in, and how should they become experts? You might like to make a list of the pluses and negatives of such people. Which are the times when you have been grateful for expertise, and which when you have resented the presence of experts? Why do we so often use the phrase 'so-called experts'? Is there a positive sort of expertise that you yourself feel you either have or could acquire?

On the Other Hand . . .

What textual communities are *not* is: institutions for the like-minded, social-welfare groups, groups of people who happen to like religious idioms and culture, escapist colonies, religious or social clubs, bitter reactionary groups who don't like the way the world has changed since their youth, or clerical fan-clubs. They are not necessarily the kind of churches which currently have a range of house groups for 'study' or which engage in education programmes. Much of what passes for Bible study in such groups is unrelated to context, uninformed about modern methods of reading the Bible, and has no clear desired outcome (that is, no one is quite sure why they do it). It is often unconnected with the rest of the church's work and activity, unrelated to worship and leads to ghetto or club mentalities. It is not connected with communication, usually being seen as individual and personal rather than community orientated and enabling. In fundamental ways this differs from the activity of the church as textual community, though I accept that this picture is a worst-case scenario, and there will be churches whose activities have a very different flavour. What I am keen to stress is that just because some people in a church seem to spend a lot of time reading and studying the Bible, this does not make them textual communities.

Similarly, engaging in an education programme does not make a church a theological community even though it may mean that that church will have a context for discussing theological issues that it may not have had before. Many such programmes pay no attention to the readers' context and give little opportunity or encouragement for the material to be adapted for local use. They sometimes come with a take-it-or-leave-it view of some Christian ideas which can border on the dogmatic, and the amount of room they leave for real discussion is questionable. Course booklets give a sense of the expert speaking from the outside. All this does is remove the place of expertise from the pulpit to the book, but not necessarily to the pew. It can also promote the view that theology is a set of agreed truths which must in some form be assented to. It is not always clear that that is only one possible definition.

Doing Theology the New Testament Way

Until now, we have concentrated for our examples on the Old Testament, but as we try to explore further what a modern textual Christian community might be like, let us take the New Testament as our model. We see there more clearly that the first Christian textual communities were not committees of scholars working out codes and constitutions which would serve the church for all time, but those who had been informed by particular contexts and experiences and who wanted to make sense of some potential answers to the 'big' questions in their situation. These are the 'exile' questions we have already identified about sin, suffering, justice, purpose, destiny, vocation, identity and God. These potential answers raised new questions such as:

Who was Jesus, how can we understand his significance, and why does it matter? The answers they came up with were framed in the language and cultural forms of each community. To Jews, Jesus could be described as the Messiah, the anointed one, and Jews would understand what that meant in relation to a long history of expectation surrounding such a figure. But that description would make little sense to non-Jews. New ways of describing Jesus' significance had to be coined for them, developed in the conviction that Jesus was as significant for non-Jews as he was for Jews. (One of the earliest decisions of the Christian community was that you didn't have to become a Jew first before you could become a Christian.) Words like 'Lord' which had a particular resonance in the Gentile world were conjured with, in order to give other communities access to the traditions about Jesus. Even within particular ethnic communities, the significance of Jesus might be interpreted differently and described differently, depending on things like whether the community was living in Jerusalem or out on the Syrian border; whether they were still in contact with Jewish synagogues or whether they had been expelled from them; whether they were accepted as Christians in their wider social communities or whether they were being harassed. This is not just true of what we might call titles of Jesus, like Messiah or Lord. It also affects what stories are told, to whom, in what way. By the incidents he chooses to include in his Gospel one writer might stress that Jesus is a miracle worker. Another might play down that aspect in favour of seeing Jesus in his role as a teacher, for example. But every time a new presentation is made it will have depended upon a huge process of selection. It will have included consideration of, for example:

- What sources are available;
- What form (miracle story, parable, debate) is most likely to communicate with the intended audience;

- What religious idioms and traditions make sense to the audience;
- How they understand those traditions;
- What particular issues are going to affect the way they hear the message.

This is actually how creative theology is done in the New Testament. What we see is that the new ways of presenting Jesus amount to new theology, new ways of talking about God, which are determined by context.

We see this even more clearly when we consider the amount of space given in the New Testament to the question: What is the church? The way in which this new kind of religious community was described, particularly in its relation to Jesus, was obviously crucial. As we have noted, no fewer than ninety-six pictures of how the church can be understood appear in the New Testament, according to Hans-Ruedi Weber,[34] and others see even more. Although they share some characteristics in common, each of them is a new attempt to relate the writer's understanding of the most significant things about the church to the readers' context, in a way that will make sense to them and inspire and excite their enthusiasm.

Reflection on Text

Have a look through the New Testament letters and see how many pictures of the church you can find. **Galatians, chapters 4, 5 and 6** will supply several examples. What do you think they have in common? Are there any that surprise you? Why do you think Paul chose these particular descriptions?

In the New Testament this is how theology of the church is

created. Familiarity has made us used to the pictures it employs, but on their first publication some of them must have seemed mind-bogglingly creative.

Paul appears to have been responsible for the description 'Body of Christ', for example. This is an exceptionally useful metaphor. It gives Christians a way of understanding their vocations. They are to continue the work Christ began on earth when he was here in bodily form. They find rationale through his *broken body* on the cross. They recall this as they share his broken *body in the Eucharist*, and declare themselves members of *his risen body* in the process. Not all pictures of the church were so successful or remain memorable, but it is a notable part of the early church's belief in itself, and its sense of adventure, that it was willing to have a shot at any number of designations. So Paul did not feel restricted to one idiom as he wrote to churches. His agenda was set by their concerns. Many of his letters have the flavour of replies, and he often speaks in those replies as one who knows the context well; as one who has visited the place or even set up the church there in the first place. So when we think how new theology is actually done, we see it on the one hand as the product of a meeting between traditions about Jesus, understood by, say, Paul in ways that he can understand, and on the other hand, the context of his addressees. Theology is what emerges from this encounter. We note two important things. The first is that Paul is essentially a practical theologian. He does not set out to write a treatise or constitution. He writes letters. He engages in a dialogue which has the effect of changing both his perceptions, which demonstrably develop over time, and those of his audience. The second is that the characteristic mode of this theological activity is *communication*. Theology happens because people want to tell other people things that they think are significant new possibilities in response to those fundamental exile questions; and because they believe they have had a new sighting of

God which has changed everything. It is not for nothing that fundamental documents of the New Testament are called 'news'.

Polemic

Readers of the New Testament will also notice that this is not the only dialogue that is being conducted. Alongside that dialogue, which seeks to explore and communicate the limits of the new potential responses to those fundamental questions, and which is creating new and daring theological forms in order to do so, there is something else. That is the polemical response to those who persist with false answers, or answers that have been superseded by the cataclysmic new events. We might compare this dialogue with that in the book of Job. Those friends speak to Job as if there is no crisis and as if the Exile hadn't happened. The conversation is heated. In New Testament times, as now, there are voices to be heard which describe Christianity as if the crucifixion hadn't happened, and that conversation can be heated too because there is a lot at stake for both sides. Christianity is not just one more religion with better rules and better rituals and more modern forms of expression. It is scandalously different from other understandings of religion, and those who write 'exilically' as we have seen Paul and the author of 1 Peter do, are among those who recognize that.

In the New Testament the arguments are with a variety of groups. There are those (who came to prominence after New Testament times) who want to claim that Christ didn't suffer. Jesus was in effect only pretending to be completely human. He was more like God just dressed up in human clothes for a while, like some store Santa Claus. In the New Testament some people think we see evidence of this argument in 1 and 2 John. A particular form of church with its own theology has emerged following the insights and style of the Gospel according to John: so far so good. However the ambiguity of that Gospel, together with its promotion of a style of church leadership that has no clear authority structure has led to this misunderstanding about the place of suffering and the relationship between God and the world; and so between Christians and the world. What came to be seen as the orthodox point of view on this is represented by 1 and 2 John. The nature of the crisis for religion lies in accepting that Jesus *did* suffer. To neglect that is to completely misunderstand the newness of Christianity. We might compare the magnitude of this mistake to that of claiming that the Holocaust never happened. Another argument is with those who want to maintain a religion based on law, and the system it presupposes. Paul is scathing on this. That kind of hope for vindication has come to an end. There is a new freedom possible (Colossians 2:14; Galatians 5:1). Connected with these are the groups who want to maintain circumcision. This for Paul is a symbol of a past system. Now there is something new. He uses some of his strongest invective in this context (Galatians 2:11–21). Then there are those who make some show of entering into the form of the new religion but without recognizing its power. The people of Corinth make a mockery of the Eucharist by the way they celebrate it, perpetuating past divisions (1 Corinthians 11:17). They abuse the whole idea of charismatic, graceful gifts by the way they misunderstand the nature of grace and squabble about them (1 Corinthians 12:1). They misrepresent baptism by treating it as the gift of the minister rather than the gift of God and they want to maintain the culture of heroes in the church which they are comfortable with in their own society (1 Corinthians 1:11–17).

Some scholars see in the Gospel of John an attempt to counter a view of the incarnation that seems to suggest that it is only partially complete. That is the view which interprets the Greek word *parousia* as looking forward to some kind of second incarnation. A case can be made that some parties in the early church misunderstood the teaching of Jesus to the extent that they believed it was possible to evade the challenge and scandal that Jesus' presence involved by pretending that there was another chance (so for example J. A. T. Robinson, *Jesus and His Coming*[35]). Jesus would revert to type and come next time as everyone had expected this time. The weak and vulnerable suffering Christ for whom traditional vindication was impossible ('He saved others, let him save himself, ho, ho, ho!') would came again in power and glory and vindicate the faithful remnant just as they anticipated. His second coming would be the big one. There are of course some sects which hold this particular belief today in that form. The Gospel of John sets out a view of the incarnation, crucifixion, resurrection and parousia that presents them as different perspectives on the one incredible, unrepeatable event. All the things necessary for salvation have happened. That is not to say that God has somehow given up or that there's nothing to ope for, of course. It is to counter a view character by denial, pretence and evasion.

The Situation Today

These do not exhaust the groups with which the New Testament takes issue but this small selection does enable us to reflect on groups, calling themselves Christian, which even today stand in denial that something cataclysmic has happened which necessitates a complete rethink. There are those today who think systems are more important than people, and whose pastoral concern consists in relating people to those systems in a way so painfully reminiscent of Job's friends that it beggars belief that they still get away with it. There are those today who think that religion is basically to do with law and keeping rules. Such people would find Islam a happier choice of religion. At least they would know where they were. There are those today who deny the importance of context and want a one-size-fits-all Christianity in the face of all the evidence that theology is not done like that. There are those for whom Christianity is best described as a repository of doctrines and dogmas – the collected wisdom of the ages. What we have to do is learn it and then believe it. There are those who have investments in other kinds of closedness and protectionism, who do not want their cosy worlds shattered or their prejudices exposed for what they are, whether they be racist or just sexually repressed. And there are those sheep in wolves' clothing who mask conservative religious agendas with trendy tunes and lively media sets. And if this sounds a little angry then so be it. Such travesties of Christianity will not characterize an exile church. That is a church straining to live with the incredible sighting of God that Jesus represents, and recognizing that nothing can be the same again, and rejoicing in that.

Reflection and Communication

A theological church has a deep interest in the traditions and an equally deep interest in the world. It hears the questions, the 'cries' as I have called them, and recognizes their seriousness and the ability of the traditions to respond to them. It lives by a continual process of reflection. It wants to communicate and sees the very action of that communication as part of its reflection. Commentary is part of its task.

As a preacher I know how valuable it is as a tool for reflection to have to answer the question: How do I communicate this? In the college where I work and where we train people for Christian ministry we use communication tasks as a means of reflection. Faced with a particular text we ask students to think about how they might communicate its message in a variety of contexts. For example:

- To children;
- To those unable to communicate, where words would be an inappropriate medium;
- To a suburban group of young families;
- In a radio thought for the day;
- As a television documentary.

What new symbols would be needed? What new examples would be required? What new stories would need to be told? What would you have to do to understand the world of the hearers? What would you need to know fully to utilize the possibilities of the different media? And when they have done this, we ask them:

- How did your understanding of the message change as the context changed?
- How did your presentation of the message change as the medium changed?
- What new understanding do you now bring to the text?
- What new theology have you done?

Reflection on Text

You might like to try this exercise with a Bible passage that means a lot to you. How would you convey its essence to a group of children, or to those with learning difficulties? What does this exercise tell you about theology? Have your views about theology changed from the beginning of the chapter?

At heart is the question what does this text *mean*, and especially what does it mean now in relation to questions that matter?

This is the culture of a theological, textual, communicating church. In a remarkable picture, Paul describes the church as a letter. 'You yourselves are our letter, written on our hearts, to be known and read by all; and you show that you are a letter of Christ, prepared by us, written not with ink but with the Spirit of the living God, not on tablets of stone but on tablets of human hearts' (2 Corinthians 3:2f.). The church can be described as a community that communicates, through its actions and through its words; through what it intends or does not intend; a community both enlivened by, and a witness to the 'aliveness' of the living God. A term which Paul uses more than anyone else in the New Testament sums it up rather well, and that is the Greek word *koinonia*. We usually translate it as fellowship, sharing or participation. It can be used to describe relations between Christians or between Christians and God. It is essentially a word which describes *connectedness*, and this is a key feature of a communicating, theological church.

This is not the place to describe the distinctive theologies of such a church (save to say that they will stand broadly in the post-exilic traditions we have outlined) because in any case they will differ. What such churches will share in common is a sense of the connectedness of all parts of that church's endeavour. It will be possible to ask of any one activity in that church how it relates to others and get a coherent answer, and that answer in turn will be related to the church's current theological understanding. To introduce a phrase like 'current theological understanding' will be to ring alarm bells in some quarters. How is authority organized in this church? Who decides what the theological understanding is? In part those are questions related to ministry, which we shall look at later. In part they raise questions about authority. The kinds of question which will be more common in a church like this are questions such as: Why are we doing this? What's in it for those who don't come? Why does this matter? How is this connected to the rest of the church? What does this amount to in practice?

The Exilic Experience

There is no shortage of books on offer which purport to give a view of what the church will be like in the twenty-first century, how its ministry will operate, and how things must change. Some of those books display such negative feelings towards the future potential of current examples and models of church life that they concentrate more on new 'ways of being church', and set about finding examples of experimental or potential Christian communities which might produce some pointers towards something better. (One has the distinct feeling that in a couple of years some of these may look rather quaint.) Some leave it at that. Others stress the need to have some way of determining whether a particular example should be termed 'church' or not. After all, surely not every group of happy, like-minded people singing religious songs and hugging each other in a community centre can be called church. The best try to work out an ecclesiology, that is a theological understanding of what the church is, or should be, which will provide a way forward, using some New Testament picture as a model. One of the most recent puts together a composite picture including: 'the called community', 'members of one body', 'a light to the nations' and 'pilgrims in progress'.[36] This is admirable but is not what I am advocating as part of the exilic experience of church. Exilic or post-exilic church is not a theological title, like 'Body of Christ'. It is a style of church which can produce such titles for itself. The paradigm of exile gives us a sense of the church's agenda, its culture, its sensitivities and its characteristic activities but does not give us the terms in which this might be communicated or articulated. That is one of the freedoms and joys of such a church. It can coin new ones. And one of the key places where it can do this is in its liturgy. Liturgy is, in the theological church, a key place of theological creativity, articulation and communication. It is also one which is participatory. This is a theme we shall explore in Chapter 8. It is only then that we shall fully be able to answer questions such as: What does it feel like to be a member of a theological or textual community, what does such a church do, and how does it differ from others?

This chapter has given partial answers to some of those questions. A modern textual community will, in addition to the general characteristics of the exilic experience church outlined already, be recognized by its:

- Sense of connectedness;
- Having an understanding of what it's about that could be called a theological rationale;
- Viewing its members as theologians;
- Dynamic view of tradition;
- Sense of its own distinctiveness;
- Awe in accepting its representative role as theological and communicative;
- Interest in liturgy and worship.

It is in these ways that a church characterized by 'settled restlessness' will display its *restlessness*. But it will also have a sense of *settledness*. It will accept that this really is home for the duration. In that way, to the casual observer it may differ little from other church communities with different understandings of their purpose. It may have jumble sales, harvest suppers, a Mothers Union, a ramblers group, crèche, luncheon club, charity shop and any other appropriate marks of a community church. Being a member of a theological church is not boring, academic or bookish or separatist. But it certainly should be interesting.

8

Come on, United

Introduction

I write as a supporter of Leeds United Football Club. In the past this experience has stood me in good stead as a preacher, particularly as you might imagine, in exemplifying endurance in the face of disillusion, or not reading too much into false dawns and the sighting of so-called green shoots. More generally, though, I have used the example of football in connection with learning about the church, and in situations where people have wanted to know how to be a church. I have told them that if you want to learn about football it is no good just reading books, and not much better listening to pundits on the TV. There is no substitute for going to a match, and being inspired to play as a result. So it is with church. There really is no substitute for going along to a match and seeing what play amounts to at its best. To learn about the church you need to experience worship.

Reflection on Experience

From your experience, what more would you have to add to that last statement to make you happy with it? Would any old service do, for example? Is it true of churches you know that joining in their worship tells you lots of positive things about them? Have you had the same experience as me, of visiting a church, on holiday perhaps, and being told, 'it's a shame you came today' because for lots of reasons today isn't typical? What kind of conclusions do you draw from this kind of reflection?

Worship and Theology

I want to claim that something happens, or at least can potentially happen, in an act of worship which is, if you like, greater than the sum of the parts. Call it the sacramental presence of God: call it the action of the Holy Spirit. There is a catalyst in worship that enables the whole thing to be dynamic rather than static, vital rather than dead, and directed rather than purposeless. I want to equate this vital heart of worship with the transaction process outlined above when we were talking about how theology is done. I want to describe the engine of worship in terms of its being part of a cycle which brings the text and tradition into contact with experience and sends them both away changed in the mind of the worshipper in a way that will lead to some new developments, which in their turn will be brought back to the worship crucible. It is this cyclical process that helps to keep worship fresh; which helps worshippers to 'see something new in the service every time I use it'. And it is through that cycle that vital links are made with what we have called practical theology.

In Chapter 6 I made the rather grand claim that it is above all in worship that practical theology is done. This might sound like nonsense. Practical theology summons pictures of active pastoral work out in the community, dealing with the casualties of the real world. Surely, you might think, worship is something of an indulgence, a privilege for the articulate few, a means of temporary escape from the rock face to a place of serenity and beauty. What could be further removed from the real world than this? I think there are three things to say here. First, that description of worship, whilst sadly recognizable, begs a lot of questions and would not describe adequately the kind of worship I have in mind. When I look at much of what passes for worship in some churches that I visit, I find myself more and more at one with the Deuteronomistic reformers of Josiah's day! Second, you will recall that our definition of practical theology was in terms of its being a way of doing theology. This approach sees theology done where religious, and particularly biblical traditions, meet and interact with experience and context in such a way that each is potentially open to transformation by the other. Its characteristic mode is reflection. This may well lead to all sorts of practical outcomes, but it is the process itself that is important for our purposes. Third, we need to remember that the word which describes worship in several Christian traditions is the word 'liturgy'. which in turn derives from a Greek word meaning 'work'. That is, liturgy and worship are not passive but active. The time of worship is a time when something happens and something is done. According to the understandings of practical theology, that 'something' includes the kind of reflection – the kind of grinding tradition against experience – that will lead to both new understandings of the tradition and new initiatives and actions in the 'real' world.

We have to be honest enough to admit that it is notoriously difficult to determine what people actually think they are doing when they worship. People do not tend to analyse for themselves what they are doing. They simply do it. Martin Stringer's recent treatment of this theme does define the questions and scholarly positions with regard to them very well.[37] The interesting question for him is: Where is the *meaning* of an act of worship to be found? Most scholars believe it to be in the text of the service, to which worshippers react. Some want to take the view that it belongs in the mind of the worshipper. The practical theology view would probably be that the meaning of an act of worship is to be discovered in the transaction between the two, that is, in the performance itself of the act of worship.

As long as they enable the process rather than disable it, there is a large variety of forms of worship ritual and liturgy which can be considered legitimate in an exilic church. In other words, this approach to worship is not limiting or determined by one particular style. Worship is in any case incredibly flexible and a huge range of human activities has throughout the ages been described in this way, including, to take a few random examples, killing both animals and humans, sexual intercourse, and eating meals. During my lifetime there have been huge changes in the styles, cultures and habits of worship. I have seen the greater emphasis on silence in some traditions, and the greater emphasis on charismatic exuberance in others. I have seen the general acceptance of unfamiliar rituals like 'passing the peace' and the popularity of new kinds of worship such as the healing service. In most churches I have witnessed a movement towards less formal language. I have seen new art forms such as dance. New and exciting architectural ideas have been related to changing ideas of what a church is for. New choreography in services is also related to changing views of ecclesiology (for example, in Anglican churches, celebrants facing the people at the altar in the Eucharist rather than facing away). These latter examples remind us that worship can adapt and respond to theological thinking. Worship can be a touchstone of where the church is at. New hymns, which are being produced at a remarkable rate, strive to catch up with what people really want to say in a way they want to say it. If the way you want to express something significant and fundamental doesn't exist, then you invent it. You find a new symbol, a new picture, a new story, a new song. It is this kind of adventurous worship-at-the-heart-of-theology that I see in the Bible's exilic churches.

Reflection on Experience

What is your attitude to new hymns? Does this bear any relation to: a) the length of time you have been going to church; b) the regularity with which you go; c) the kinds of occasion on which you go? What other circumstances have affected your answer. Try to think of a hymn written within the last twenty years that has had a really positive effect on you, perhaps helping you to make more contemporary connections with religious ideas. What made that hymn so good? Do you recognize this as a piece of theology?

Worship and Theology as Old Testament Exilic Experience

It is no accident, I think, that key responses to the crises of exile in both Old and New Testaments place importance on worship. We have seen how, in the Old Testament, the D writers began with a complete overhaul of the worship experience. Their aim, in part at least, was to persuade a sceptical public that worship was actually about things that matter, and not just a case of doing something because 'our ancestors did and it's a way of maintaining our identity'. Worship is not something for the folk museum and heritage trail, they said. It has to be at the heart of life, dealing with questions of life and death. The real nub of separate identity lies with the Covenant relationship and worship has to be about how that is taken seriously and how it works out in practice. So they devised new services, making very clear that these were completely different from what might have passed for worship before (Deuteronomy 12:2–7).

Later on, the P writers made institutional liturgical life a key item of their programme for religious continuity and development. Through that emphasis, not only were they able to introduce a more mystical reflective style into theological statements such as that of Genesis 1, but they were able also in their own way to relate Covenant and Election and other traditional theological terms to current experience. Through their particular view of the temple and its life, they were able also to describe the vision they had of how things needed to change. Their solution to the perception of God's absence, a key theological, post-Exile question, was to find ways of asserting God's 'sacramental' presence in worship. Worship could therefore include statements about destiny and eschatology, and worshippers could almost be encouraged to live 'as if' the temple and its life were a foretaste of that greater connectedness and forgiveness still to come. Worship provided the context for that 'as-ifness', that foretaste.

Walter Brueggemann has suggested that in the book of Psalms we see a psychological movement, which could be interpreted against a background of exile experience, though he himself does not press this application.[38] He divides the psalms into three groups. The first groups he calls 'psalms of orientation'. These are the psalms which 'express a confident, serene settlement of faith issues. Some things are settled and beyond doubt, so that one does not live and believe in the midst of overwhelming anxiety'.[39] These are psalms which it is possible to use only before great dislocation has shattered belief in a God who has ordered all things well. They have a creation style of theology, emphasizing security and a sense of boundaries and certainties. Such a style is particularly suitable for children who need to learn about the world in a trusting way. It might also be suitable for those who have not experienced the anguish of exile. However, they are unsuitable for uncritical use with experienced people. Those who can happily sing 'All Things Bright and Beautiful' in a world where so many people are suffering pointlessly and need-lessly are doing something inappropriate, on the face of it. That something becomes even worse if we find that the singer has every reason to believe what he or she is singing. To hear successful, western, white males thanking God for all he has done for them, and what a great job he has made of creating such a wonderful world is nothing short of obscene.

The second group of psalms Brueggemann calls 'psalms of disorientation'. They are those psalms of lament which describe the way in which such old certainties were shat-tered, perhaps by exile, perhaps in some other exile-like experience of the kinds we have been exploring. These psalms give a measure of what has been lost in the experi-ence. They exhibit disillusion, anger, despair, hopelessness, emptiness. These are appropriate psalms for a very large number of the world's population. And yet, as Brueggemann wryly comments: 'It is a curious fact that the church has, by and large, continued to sing songs of orientation in a world increasingly experienced as disoriented.'[40] He sees this as one of those acts of denial which, we have noticed, always appears to accompany exile. The church can use psalms of orientation with integrity nowadays in the West only if it uses them as a way of asserting trust in the face of the evidence. An expression of what he means is to be found at Habakkuk 3:18. Here the prophet outlines a long list of things that have gone wrong. For those who want the kind of faith that depends upon results here is ample opportunity to give up – the classic exile predicament. What Habakkuk does is different though. He asserts that he will still believe *despite* the evidence. Given the facts, *yet* he will believe, *nevertheless* he will believe. (Perhaps being a Leeds United supporter is a better preparation for discipleship than I had thought.) Brueggemann calls this 'the bold nevertheless'.[41] Churches which use orientation psalms in full knowledge of failure and disaster and whose faith is not based on a god of good results can do so with a clear conscience.

A third category is those hymns and songs of thanks-giving which he calls, 'psalms of new orientation'. These are the psalms whose users have reflected upon the catas-trophe and know there is no going back. New theology is needed. It is a theology which, like the best post-exilic theology, recognizes something new and wondrous about God that demands a new response.

> The speaker and the community of faith are often surprised by grace, when there emerges in present life a new possibility that is inexplicable, neither derived nor extrapolated, but wrought by the inscrutable power and goodness of God. We do not know how such a newness happens any more than we know how a dead person is raised to new life, how a leper is cleansed, or how a blind person can see.[42]

Reflection on Text

If you would like to see the differences between the kinds of psalm that Brueggemann suggests, then some good examples are: psalms of orientation, **8, 33, 145**; psalms of disorientation, **13, 88, 137**; psalms of new orientation, **34, 65, 124**. It is of course par-ticularly helpful to read them with the aid of Brueggemann's own commentary.

Reflecting on this we might make the following points:

- Although it may not be historically permissible to equate particular psalms with particular historic stages in the process of exile and return (for an attempt to do this see Michael Goulder[43]), there is a strong resemblance between the three stages Brueggemann identifies and the movement we have seen in the theological expressions of those who have reflected on the process of exile.
- Brueggemann's analysis reminds us that congregations are not homogenous. In any particular congregation at any time there will be those who inhabit each of the different stages he identifies. This is an important insight for those responsible for leading worship.
- His work reminds us of the local creativity evidenced by the Psalms, and of the importance of communal response.
- His work helps us to read the Psalms as a commentary on the human experience of coming to terms with exile from the standpoint of that community of faith which continues to trust and perhaps to utter the 'bold nevertheless' of Habakkuk.

From the Old Testament, then, we could say that we see the importance of worship for exiles set out in two ways. From the D and P writings we see that worship provides a new grammar for theology. It provides new categories, new forms of expression, a new forum for ideas. It also, secondly, helps set up new institutions within which those ideas can best be expressed and the necessary post-exilic theological reflection can take place. Even the book of Job, which relies so much on cerebral argument, is finally resolved only in a context of worship as Job ministers to his friends as they bring their sacrifices.

Things that Matter

From time to time, in the college where I teach, groups of students are encouraged to design services of worship as a collaborative activity. Often these are arranged to coincide with some festival of the church, but occasionally when we have run out of saints (even Welsh saints) or events in the Christian calendar, groups simply arrange services according to a theme they all agree on, such as healing or penitence or justice. I was present recently at a preliminary discussion with one of these groups who couldn't seem to find a suitable satisfying theme for such a service, when someone suggested: 'Let's just take as our theme: things that matter.' And so they did. And it was very good. Each of the dozen or so participants had to think about the things that really mattered to them, and to find a way of relating them to the practice of Christian worship, either through reading, testimony, prayer, dance, hymn or in some other way. The contributions were varied. Some were to do with the area of vocation and gifts. A musician demonstrated the importance of music in her life, a parent brought along photos of the family. That crossed into the area of relationships, which almost inevitably showed up areas where forgiveness seemed necessary. One person spoke about an unresolved estrangement with one of their (grown-up) children. That sense of unresolvedness seemed to move us naturally towards questions of justice and peace, and different members described situations in the world or in society that mattered to them for different reasons. Afterwards, members of the congregation spoke of how well they had been able to identify with the issues raised and how it had helped them to face questions in the reflective opportunities that were built into the service.

In that exercise we were, I believe, demonstrating some of the key things about being a textual community, and by extension an exilic community. First, we were asserting that worship has to be about things that matter. In these new times worship cannot be peripheral. It cannot be an entertainment. Neither can it be serious stuff in the way it used to be before the exile. We can no longer believe in a

God who will make it rain if we perform the right ritual, or who will bless the faithful with success or who will forgive and cleanse our community if we offer the right sacrifice. Once upon a time worshippers could be serious in that way. Then, worship was certainly about things that mattered, but those days have gone, and something has to be salvaged from the wreckage. The exile itself has helped define for us the things that matter. They are the questions of identity, vocation, destiny, suffering, justice, relationship and forgiveness – and our students' choices reflected that. But second, the service was giving participants access to the treatment of those questions in a personal and communal way. It was helping them to engage with the things that matter in a liturgical setting that enabled those questions to collide with traditional resources, such as the Bible and the Christian spiritual and liturgical heritage. That has been the experience of exilic and especially post-exilic communities throughout the ages. Textual communities need some way in which to demonstrate their new theology, and in a situation where the canon of scripture is closed, then worship is the obvious place where this can happen. Liturgy helps both to create and to demonstrate theology.

Reflection on Experience and Text

If you were to put together a service with the title, 'things that matter', what would it include? This is a particularly good exercise to do as a group. What biblical resources would you choose to interact with the things that matter to you?

Worship and Theology as New Testament Exilic Experience

It might be thought that the New Testament offers less opportunity for discussion of how worship operates in a church of exiles, but perhaps that letter addressed to exiles, 1 Peter, may prove helpful.

The letter contains so many allusions to worship that some commentators have in the past taken the view that it was itself a complete liturgy. In terms of our analysis of textual exilic responses this is an understandable mistake. The things that need to be said lend themselves so readily to expression through worship. Indeed they are often so new that only the radical creativity of worship can communicate them fully, and they are so profound and biographically significant that only worship can carry the emotional baggage necessary to respond. It should come as no surprise, then, to find allusions to worship in exilic churches. The letter is also a very short document which needs to take account of the addressees' awareness of the experience of suffering. So in 1 Peter worship and suffering are brought into sharp juxtaposition,which is theologically creative. If it is true that current suffering is to be made sense of in terms of the relationship between the suffering believer and the suffering Christ, then only worship can begin to make such a claim either credible or manageable. Those addressed have to enter a realm which might be described as 'mystical' in order to contemplate how this relationship might work. That is not to divorce it from the practical theology–worship cycle we described above; indeed quite the opposite. Here, believers who are suffering are brought into contact with a piece of theology/text/tradition which gives them a new tool for reflecting on their experience. That reflection, in turn, might lead both to a new, more positive attitude of fortitude or submission towards the suffering and a new assessment of the nature of Jesus.

The cry to make sense of suffering is also that cry to make sense of God which we have come to recognize as part of the exilic tradition. In this case the scandalous thing about the new sighting of God is precisely to do with his suffering. There are other familiar cries. There is the *cry to authenticate this new sighting of God*. Just as the Old Testament people could rely on the word of the prophet, so people in the New Testament need an authoritative voice. This is provided in 1 Peter by the designation of the author as Peter the Apostle – a designation many scholars believe to be historically untrue. Nevertheless this author speaks with the authority of Peter in his role as a witness of the sufferings of Christ (5:1). Another familiar cry is about *identity*. As we saw in the response of the P and D traditions, exiles need to be assured of who they were, and whom they might be, and of the continuity between the two. Worship and the cultus were key ingredients in the scripting of answers. So it is in 1 Peter. Effectively, to put it at its bluntest, what is needed is to *reinvent* the cultus for these new times, and to *invent* baptism.

The reinvention of the cultus is seen most clearly in 1 Peter 2:4–10. Here the epithets once considered copyright to Israel are applied to the new Christian community, but more than that. The cultus around which this Israelite/Jewish identity revolved is now completely reimagined. The temple is no longer a building. It is now a community. That community is capable of carrying out the functions which were once sacred to a separate caste of priests. The key task of offering sacrifices has now been re-expressed as offering spiritual sacrifices. It follows that the whole notion of priesthood, and of the relations of the priest to the community and the community to God need to be rethought. Worship in this church, assured of its continuity with the past, will nevertheless have a lot of exciting theological reflecting to do, but now it has a new permission to do it.

Just as the P writers accepted the permission to be

innovative in their day with the traditions about male circumcision, giving something which was probably commonplace a new dimension and meaning, so the author of 1 Peter can join the New Testament enterprise with regard to the innovation of baptism. That too is to become a distinctive mark of belonging. It is to become a sign of protection and ownership for those who trust in God without looking for results, and who are prepared to utter a 'bold nevertheless' in the face of suffering. Other cries are responded to through the idiom of this new baptism as the author himself explores its potential as a symbol and metaphor of the relationship between the believer and the suffering saviour. These include the cries about whether the Covenant is still valid – *the call for assurances about appropriate behaviour*. They include also the *cry about the problem of overcoming evil*, and whether this new sighting has meant that issues of destiny and vision have to be revisited. They also include the questions about *sin* and whether *forgiveness* has become more possible now. We imagine this community exploring with its correspondent, its theological consultant, how baptism can become a context for the consideration of and response to these cries. And we do so remembering that this is not some academic pursuit or training exercise but something which springs from deep personal need and pastoral involvement. This is practical theology.

Within the idiom of baptism 1 Peter finds it possible to underwrite the significance of this time. It makes all things possible. Baptism is connected with new life, new birth and a new name, these in turn are connected with the death and resurrection of Christ (1:3, 21, 23, 2:2, 3:21, 4:16). Baptism allows us to find a new metaphor for protection (1:5, 5:6f.). Baptism is a kind of witness, it is a public declaration, but that word 'witness' is related to the word 'martyr', connecting the believer to the expectation of suffering (1:6f.). Holiness is characteristic of the baptized, as it was demanded in the Holiness Code in the P tradition, from which 1 Peter quotes, of the first post-exiles (1:15f., 1:22, 2:2, 11). Just as those people had to come to terms with a new ecumenical picture of God, so in 1 Peter, baptism is the entrance to a universal community (1:17, 5:9). Baptism confers membership and demands a new mutuality (1:22, 2:5, 10, 3:8, 4:8–11, 5:5). The issue of sin is acknowledged and connected with the story of Jesus, which is told in a new way to enable the link to be made in what will become a liturgical creed and later text (2:21–24, 3:13–18, 4:13). The message is also carried by these stories, as it was by the D histories: Do not expect life to be fair, but endure it and trust. And so, finally, questions of destiny and what may be hoped for can also be addressed in this context (1:4, 7, 4:7, 17, 5:1, 10). In 1 Peter an excellent example is provided of how a Christian congregation can begin to grapple with the significant questions in these new times, and express their responses and explorations in the idiom of worship.

Reflection on Text

Look up the references to **1 Peter** in the paragraph above and think about them in the framework of 'inventing baptism'. Has this added anything new to your understanding of baptism?

We might note two other things before we leave 1 Peter. First, alongside these examples of restless creativity there is evidence of settledness. This is not a community – despite the end of all things being at hand (4:7) – which is un-concerned about appropriate behaviour in a settled com-munity of wives, husbands, masters and slaves (2:13–17, 3:1–7). There is no evidence that the congregation addres-sed is awaiting some imminent revolution which will reverse the earthly order. Also notable is what 1 Peter has to say about the cultus in 2:4–9, in that it affirms the priestly *function* but demands a rewrite of the *custom and practice* which has characterized it up until now. The movement is generally in the direction away from the individual and towards the community. Even if, in the future, individuals do carry out cultic functions, they will do so with a new mandate, as representatives of that community, acting on its behalf and doing in the name of the community that which the community is qualified to do, rather than on the basis of some specially conferred status unrelated to the authority of the community.

Conclusion

In a brief chapter such as this it would be impossible to say everything that ought to be said about worship. Our aim is much more limited, namely to ask: What can we, in our modern situation, take from the exilic churches' experience of worship-at-the-heart-of-theology? First, we might note *an attitude that worship matters*. Worship is perhaps the only place where theological newness can be assimilated into the life of the church, especially once the canon of sacred scripture was declared closed and the Bible itself was complete. How then were future sightings to be affirmed, authenticated and reflected upon, but through worship? A carelessness about worship may indeed signify a church that is theologically moribund. Second, we might note *a style which is flexible, open and adventurous*. This does not mean that all order in worship is abandoned in favour of something impromptu. What it does mean is that congregations should not consider themselves slaves to a liturgy, and anxious with regard to their response to it. They need to feel at ease with it. This is also an activity which demands the provisionality we have noted before. The as-ifness of worship acknowledges the incompleteness of our knowledge of God, whilst its sacramental acts assure us by his presence.

The kind of phrases which have cropped up throughout our exploration of this theme give the sense of what this style of worship needs to achieve. It needs to be able to be theologically subversive, to have creative possibility, to be exploratory and innovative with an awareness of its provisionality. Worship too is for the time being. It needs to convey newness; to tell stories in a fresh way that recount the sightings of God and that make the appropriate connections with our lives. It needs to help us feel that we are relating, rather than being systematized or institutional-ized. It needs to include the kinds of art forms or genres that are sufficiently open and ambiguous to invite creative reflection rather than close it off; that enable the articula-tion of dream and vision. Crucially it needs to find convinc-ing ways of asserting God's presence, especially in response to those for whom all the evidence in their experience points to God's absence. In some churches this will be conveyed through sacraments and symbols, in others through charismatic demonstrations, in others through invocations of praise. Such kinds of preference are not crucial and not what I mean by style.

Third, exilic churches should have *an idiom which is participatory*, and which allows the access that will enable reflection to happen and new theology to be created most authentically. It would make a mockery of all that we have said about church membership and characteristic activity if it were the case that at the last, all decisions about wor-ship and other church work were taken by a powerful individual or oligarchy. Finally, they will be *characterized by connectedness*. Worship will be seen as one part of a theological enterprise which has other parts called church order, church ministry, church service in the world, mission and evangelism. Perhaps in the end, 'connected' is a better title for a church than 'united'.

9

For the Time Being

Some years ago, at a conference called Easter People, participants were invited to visit seven different churches in the town where the conference was held (Bournemouth UK), each of which had been designed, for the period of the conference, as an example of a possible model for the church of the future. They included 'the church of the arts' and 'the church of the open door' as examples. One church model that was not included was 'the church of the exile experience'. But what might such a church have looked like had it been included? What would it be like to be a member of such a church?

Reflection on Experience

Based on our treatment of this theme so far how would you set out 'a church of the exile' for an exhibition of this kind. How would you best describe what was different about it? You might think of the use of

- notice boards
- visual displays
- banners
- if the furniture isn't fixed, opportunities for re-ordering

- availability of church publicity material

What would be the best way to convey the essence of the exilic experience?

Had you asked me that question before I wrote this book I might have given a very different answer from the one I now offer. Simply reflecting on what 'exile' usually means nowadays, I would probably have given a response, very much like some contemporary American ones, which would have emphasized the distinctiveness of the church set in an alien culture. I have now come to see that the essence of the exile experience lies elsewhere. It lies rather in the development of textual communities; exilic churches if you like, characterized by their practical theological creativity.

1. Connectedness is one important feature of an exilic church. Textual communities are almost always keen to interpret themselves to the world, and that is one way of recognizing them. They are keen to find ways of explaining what they do and why they do it, and by implication why others might want to do it. Churches that are good at this have the following characteristics.

First, they will understand the importance of invitation to, and opportunity for, dialogue. It is likely, for example, that they will have good relations with the local schools. Probably, both the local comprehensive and primary schools will send classes to the church regularly as part of their curriculum requirements, to learn more about vestments and worship, to do church trails, to see dolls baptized and so on. These churches will look for opportunities to make it easy for people to enter the building. They will hold special non-threatening, user-friendly events such as open-days or exhibitions. They will recognize that a theological community needs dialogue partners.

Second, more than simply getting people in, these churches will have worked at ways of communicating with those who respond to the invitation, which convey the essence of the church community truthfully. This may mean the production of visual materials, church trails, videos, games and so on. It will also mean that a wide variety of people will be involved in the presentations to such guests in order to convey the sense of participation that such a church invariably has. It will involve a care about what symbols are used in church, what music used, what other media employed. The choice of these materials will demonstrate a church which shows real interest in those who are not its members, and a real commitment to listening to them, and speaking with them.

Third, there will be a sense in such churches that the programmes, the materials, symbols and so on have been worked out and are owned, not just inherited.

Fourth, such churches are generally proactive. As a resident in a place which has such a church you will always have a good chance of knowing what it is doing. And that is not just because it will be good at publicity (which is usually true), but also because what it does is so interesting and will coincide with non-church agendas so closely that you will want to take notice of it. It will be a talking point, if not a matter of local pride, even among those who are not its members. It may be that the church is used for the production of some thought-provoking piece of drama or as a setting for an 'Any Questions'-style panel evening with interesting and unpredictable guests, or it may be that the church is acting as co-ordinator for some local campaign which raises justice issues.

Lying behind all this is theological activity which is concerned about what the church is for, and which has at least concluded that it is meant to be at home in its setting whilst being aware that 'being at home' includes a responsi-bility to theological dialogue which includes an awareness of a special identity and commission. Such a church has the confidence to open dialogue, the humility to listen, the interest to care and the sympathy, born of the experience of exile, to be attractive.

2. It follows from this that textual communities have a particular interest in the theological category of ecclesiology. As pragmatists they are interested in answers to the question: What is the church for? One of the most widely used Lenten courses over the last twenty years in Britain was that produced by the British Council of Churches in 1985 with the title, *What on Earth is the Church For?*[44] It elicited so many responses they were subsequently published. The textual community recognizes the currency of this question and does not feel bound by existing categories in which to express answers. We have referred to Hans-Ruedi Weber's claim that there are ninety-six pictures of the church contained in the New Testament. This claim is made in the context of the kind of Bible study that would appeal most to the textual community. Weber interprets the biblical tradition by outlining characteristics that these pictures have in common. All show a connectedness with Jesus. All show a connectedness with the world. All display some understanding of connectedness within the Christian community. When he actually conducts this study, Weber then invites participants to go for a walk and observe, and if possible bring back, some new symbol which, for them, speaks of what the church might be in their context. A textual community is always on the lookout for the new, and aware of its theological responsibility.

A simple example which will be familiar to many is the search for a logo. I remember being part of a church which had a lively ramblers group. It was one of the strategic ways of bringing together different parts of the church and helping them to get to know one another better. Members decided that it would be good to have a group sweatshirt.

The question was, what sort of design should it contain? It transpired on wider enquiry that one of the youth groups had been having the same thought, as had the Sunday School. Members of the church who organized the local old-people's luncheon club also wanted some kind of shirt they could wear which would give them some kind of corporate identity. Clearly, what was needed was a church shirt. But it must have a logo, and what was that to be? In the end we organized a competition among some of the younger members that was judged by some of the older ones to come up with something everyone acknowledged and would feel at home wearing. Though this is a familiar example, which on the face of it seems quite banal, it is actually no less theologically profound than ecclesiological statements in the New Testament, and can be judged according to similar criteria. Certainly similar questions will go into the process of design, such as: What does the logo need to say? What aspect of church life should it highlight? Who will have to recognize it? What do we want people to think when they see it? Is it possible to translate our ideas about ourselves into this new medium?

Reflection on Text and Experience

If you are a member of a church what kind of logo would you design for its members? Would the logo describe the church as it is or as you would want it to be? You may well find that you want to include some symbols which relate to the Christian tradition, such as crosses, churches or doves, for example. You may also find that you want to include some pictures or symbols which refer to the locality. Which ones would you choose and why? What does the whole process tell you about communicating messages, and doing theology?

3. I have stressed in various places that the style of a textual community is participative as well as connected, and that it delights in doing theology, in a reflective way that has real outcomes. An example of what this can mean in practice is provided by a church just a short distance away from where I am now writing in Auckland, New Zealand, at the Anglican church of St Luke in Mount Albert. This church has developed a group of young people aged from ten to fifteen who are called the 'Thomas Group'. The group has a certain amount of cachet amongst young people in the church who are anxious to join it when they are old enough. The group is commissioned each year as its membership changes, in a congregational setting. Among the words used are these: 'You are the Thomas's amongst us. You are to reach out and touch; to ask the doubting questions; to explore the unexplored.' The group meets monthly, at the time of the Eucharist service in church, which they rejoin at the Offertory. Their adult leader introduces one of the readings for the day, juxtaposed with some striking example of contemporary experience designed to foster reflection. As the group reflect and discuss together, their aim is to produce a question for the congregation. This question is delivered just before the congregation leaves church with the words 'The Thomas question for the community this week is . . .' That question is reprinted each remaining week of the month in the parish magazine. One recent example, a reflection on Matthew 18:21ff., was: 'Why is it that Christians who know about forgiveness ask for longer sentences and capital punishment for criminal offenders?' The question was asked in the spirit of: 'Please help us to understand this because it makes no sense to us.' On another occasion the group interviewed a homeless man who was living in the vicinity of the church premises,

which he often frequented, in order to frame a question along the lines of: 'Why is the community so afraid of this man when he seems to us to have no power, and when we are only afraid *for* him as a vulnerable person?'

Reflection on Text

Imagine yourself as leader of a Thomas Group. The passage for reflection is part of the Passion story, perhaps **Luke 23:1–25**. What materials might you choose to illuminate the meaning of the passage for the group today? What questions might you expect to emerge? How important would it be to allow unexpected questions to be asked? Do you think this is a useful exercise? Can you imagine it working in settings with which you are familiar?

The Thomas question is not treated patronizingly by the church. Informal conversations about it are normal, and there is an expectation of further dialogue. Through the work of the group, the wider church is encouraged to challenge its own presuppositions on the one hand; and find ways of framing sincerely held beliefs in a way that will convey them adequately to this age group, on the other ('This is why we . . .'). The Thomas question can on occasion appear on the agendas of other church groups, and indeed can influence church policy. One Thomas question about illiteracy, for example, led to the church's developing an outreach literacy project. This is what is meant by connectedness, participation, and the kind of reflection that changes things. Is there anyone reading this who would not like to be part of such a church? People want to be theologians, want to allow the text to work on their lives and want to make a difference. They want to feel part of a community which honours that vision. The Thomas group is exilic because it deals with the big questions; deals with them in this open way; expects what it does to lead to fresh theology, and is interested in communicating what it comes up with. It is in that sense that textual communities have a sense of being mature religious communities. To enter them does not feel like entering something designed for children, in which adults are allowed to participate under certain conditions, one of which is the suspension of normal critical judgement, and the suppression of adult experience and response.

4. Textual communities have a sense of place. That is an inevitable consequence of exile. One of the effects of exile is to make one sensitive to place. If one grows up in a place and simply inherits it, one will have a different view of it from those who come to it as exiles. Sometimes one will undervalue it and take it for granted: sometimes overvalue and romanticize it. But exiles always come to someone else's land and have to negotiate their own place within it. And that means learning about how the place is perceived by all those who claim to have some stake in it. That is the extent to which the idea of the church set in a different culture has creative possibility, but that possibility will often be expressed more in terms of courtesy than hostility. Place is also essential to theology. Theology needs a context and it cannot always be done on the move. In New Zealand, no less than in Wales, there are complex cultural issues about whose the land actually is, and a practical theologian would say that no one could possibly minister successfully in such an environment without sensitivity to that, and all that it involves in terms of language and idiom. Other approaches would be tantamount to theological colonialism, exhibiting not the vulnerability and tentativeness of questioning exiles, but rather the brash certainties of a conquering, powerful

establishment. The task of enabling a church to reflect its place is a theological one that a textual community relishes.

The (Anglican) Church of New Zealand Prayer Book includes in its devotions for Monday mornings, a song of praise called 'Benedicite Aotearoa'. Many people will be familiar with a similar hymn of praise based on Apocryphal additions to the book of Daniel, which was set as an alternative to the Te Deum Laudamus in the 1662 Prayer Book. The biblical setting for the hymn was the point in the book of Daniel (between 3:23 and 3:24) where the three young men were cast into the fiery furnace only to emerge unscathed. It is an exile setting: 'For we O Lord have become fewer than any other nation, and are brought low this day in all the world because of our sins. In our day we have no ruler, or prophet or leader, no burnt offering or sacrifice, or oblation, or incense, no place to make an offering before you and to find mercy' (Prayer of Azariah 1:14f.). God's protection, which all those cultic institutions and people might have been designed to secure under the old dispensation, is demonstrated as being possible even without them. This leads to a hymn of praise which is meant to be totally ecumenical, communicating that new sense of God's greatness and freedom that is characteristic of exile writing. What the compilers of the New Zealand Prayer Book have done is to give that same hymn a sense of locality, to make it 'our' hymn rather than 'theirs'. So it includes such sentiments as:

You kauri and pine, rata and kowhai, mosses and ferns: Give to our God your thanks and praise.

And

You Maori and Pakeha, women and men, all who inhabit the long white cloud: Give to our God your thanks and praise.

The compilation of such a text is a theological task. It involves the consideration and rejection of some phrases as inappropriate and others as appropriate. That matter of judgement is based both on the kind of theological understanding that is courteous enough to place women before men; and on a careful listening to the context that enables unfamiliar words like Pakeha (meaning those of European settler stock) to be used correctly. This task also betrays a particularly adventurous approach to liturgy, and hence theology which is typical of textual communities. It is not afraid.

Reflection on Text

Imagine setting out to write a 'Benedicite' for your setting. What would it give thanks for? What local allusions would earth it and make it 'yours'? If you do this as a group activity, it would be good to start on your own and then compare suggestions before moving on together. How helpful do you think it really is to have liturgy which is local in this way?

5. Allied to this kind of sensitivity, is a sensitivity about God born of what might be called, a love at first absence. Just as one can take for granted a place in which one has grown up, so one can take for granted the God with whom one grew up, and cease to be interested in exploration about that God. For those who do not fall prey to despair and atheism, exile actually breeds a new interest in questions about God and a new robustness in pursuing them.

6. Textual communities are prepared to offer commentary. We have already noted that they are prepared to interpret

the church to the world. They are prepared to go further. They are prepared to offer a Christian perspective, and possibly critique, on secular activities in society. This is a legitimate sense in which churches can engage in the activity sometimes referred to as 'civic religion'. At one end of the scale we see a church that is happy to play host to the Annual Service of the Hospital League of Friends, or Rotary, or the Young Farmers Club. Such occasions give the church opportunity to find appropriate symbols, texts and liturgies to open meaningful dialogue with these groups which will give everyone something to think about. At the other end we have the possibly more controversial use of churches for national and civic ceremonial such as Remembrance Sunday, or Mayor's Sunday, or a service at the start of the Assize sessions. The textual community sees these as challenging opportunities both for service, witness and learning. It does not feel compromised or tainted by opening dialogue with groups who, on the face of it, may appear to have little Christian commitment. Such occasions force the community to recognize the realities of the situation in which it is set, and perhaps the alternative 'take' on issues of war, power and justice which some groups present may represent.

7. That being said, textual communities are aware of the danger of becoming Babylonian. At the end of the book of Job, religious rituals are still observed and indeed are necessary to resolve the issue of the book. To a casual observer it could seem that nothing has changed, and yet everything has changed. Exilic churches are aware that a lot of their activities may appear to the casual observer indistinguishable from the kinds of directionless church that was little more than a civic institution, so criticized by American writers. To that extent they have a particular interest in questions of identity. I have suggested that it is largely inappropriate in the West to speak of a church *in*

exile. That allows us no way of speaking meaningfully about the real exile of churches in other parts of the world. I have preferred to speak of churches *for exiles*. In such churches, the negotiations have already taken place that enable the community to be in some respects at home, and in others restless and rootless. As in the examples of biblical exilic responses and communities that we have looked at, such negotiations have resulted in distinctive identity being expressed through the institutions of worship, and through alternative forms of community life. The settledness has enabled real, creative, contextual theology to be done. Withdrawal into a ghetto on the one hand, or routine and predictable criticism of society on the other, have both been rejected. Worship is the main distinctive thing about Christian communities. To an extent it is fair to say that that is what churches are for, though that needs a lot of further explanation. Exilic churches, and textual communities for whom worship is so important in reflective cycles, are happy to be defined both by their worship and their conscious or unconscious exhibition of alternative forms of community life.

8. Textual churches in the exilic tradition give special priority to certain theological categories. Chief amongst them are the scandal of suffering, the problem of overcoming evil, and the necessity of forgiveness. Exilic churches are pastorally aware, conscious that suffering is the thing that has brought many of the members together. Forgiveness will be a major motif of its pastoral approach, and the overcoming of evil will maintain its vision and hope. We have already noted that in 1 Peter, worship and suffering are closely connected in an exilic church. So it is today. Exilic churches are serious about suffering. This too is an issue for worship. As early as the New Testament itself there is evidence that when worship became too divorced from suffering some people began to get concerned. This

was particularly an issue as far as the Eucharist was concerned.

In some churches, clearly, the fellowship aspect of the meal had become divorced from the commemoration of Christ's suffering. In the exilic church of 1 Peter we see the importance of finding ways of connecting believers and their suffering with that of Christ, but not only 1 Peter shows such a concern. In Corinth Paul has to remind Christians there about two things to do with the Eucharist. First, that as a fellowship meal it has to reflect something that is real and not just hypothetical. It cannot simply reflect the class divisions of Corinthian society (1 Corinthians 11:20–22). But in addition to that, the Eucharist in Corinth has lost its edge. It does not have suffering at its core (11:26). One interpretation of the Emmaus road journey in Luke 24 would see it as affirming the necessary understanding that 'the Messiah should suffer' before his presence at the Eucharist can be recognized (24:26). Not every social occasion at which Christians are present, involving food, is a Eucharist. Textual communities today will see the Eucharist as much more than a happy get-together for Christians. They will recognize that Christ's presence means taking his suffering seriously, and this will be one of the ways in which they are able to make connections with a suffering world, and so to give the occasion theological reflective potential.

Reflection on Text

Read the story of the journey to Emmaus in **Luke 24:1–35**, and think of it as a kind of parable being written by someone in answer to the question: What kind of mystical meeting with Jesus is a Eucharist? Is this a useful perspective for you on the text?

What might the answer to the question be, do you think?

9. As one might expect then, textual communities have a particular approach to ministry. In a community that is connected, reflective, liturgical, overtly theological and committed to access and participation, the role of the ordained minister will be crucial. My preferred term for this person is 'parish theologian' or perhaps 'community theologian'. The key role here is to enable the community to operate as a theological community, primarily through training, encouraging and enabling members to be participants in the theological task. This kind of leadership might traditionally be described as 'episcopal', that is, to do with oversight. It will involve offering commentary both on traditions by which experience might be interpreted, and on the situations in the world which might lead to a new understanding or even development in the traditions, but especially it will mean imparting the skills and sharing the power which will enable the community to do this for itself. To that end the minister's role involves both taking responsibility and being subversive. Such a person must have a strong sense of the importance of being a communicator and have a degree of multi-lingualism with regard to modes of Christian expression. It will be this minister who enables the necessary sense of interconnectedness to develop.

As we have seen, in exilic churches ministers, ordained or otherwise, will need particular sensitivity to the cries of isolation, marginalization, frustration, God-forsakenness and despair and be able to alert congregations to them. They will need to understand the tradition of exile in which they stand and so offer words both of judgement and hope, looking for the parables which vitalize and flesh out the biblical revelation in terms of contemporary life and experience. They need to inspire congregations to want to participate in the great adventure of theology, and to model the kind of reflective practice which will make this possible.

This minister needs to search for sightings of God in unusual places, with a due sense of humility, and the ability to communicate honestly to the congregation what they have found.

All of these are pointers, signposts towards what life in a textual Christian community might be like. These congregations stand in a tradition which is traceable back to the Old Testament Exile, and in our view are its most authentic modern counterparts.

Exile and the Church

This study has had two starting points. The first was the desire to find a way of reading the Old Testament today that enables us to see it as a whole and to get a handle on it. Bearing in mind the directions of critical scholarship generally, and Old Testament scholarship in particular, I set out a view of how the Old Testament might be considered as a series of writings occasioned by the experience of Exile, including its anticipation and aftermath; and then set about wondering if this had any implications for the contemporary practice of faith. Second though, I have noted a tendency among some modern writers to favour the term 'exilic' to describe contemporary modes of church life, and I have wondered what that might mean and how we might judge the application; aware that 'exilic' is a term like 'Celtic Christianity' that can mean almost anything you want it to mean. To help us reach a judgement we looked also at the New Testament. I noted that just as, on one understanding, the Exile effectively provided the trigger for huge textual activity which came to be our Old Testament, so the crucifixion of Jesus could be seen as the trigger for the textual activity which led to the formation of the New Testament.

Our study has suggested that 'exilic' can describe a mode of church life that is, in my view, both authentic and desirable, based on the idea of the 'textual community'. This I have described as a place in which particular conditions of ecclesiology, worship and ministry combine to enable creative theology to be done. This theology is not divorced from the practical tasks and responsibilities of church life. Indeed the opposite is true. Such communities in a sense embody the tenets of what in modern times we have come to call practical theology. I have supplied some suggestions, pointers and signposts to enable clearer discernment of what membership of such communities involves and how they may be recognized. It will be clear from the lists and examples given that exilic churches are indeed to be found. They may not be the majority but they do exist and it is possible for others to be like them without the major rewriting that some visions of the church in the future seem to presuppose. Implications of this view include the following.

First, I have noted the proliferation of current studies of how ministry, or the church might develop in the future. If I am correct in my analysis, it will be clear that many of these start in the wrong place. They feel bound by existing categories of theological, and especially ecclesiological description. They describe no mechanism by which the new theological thinking, through which alone church life will be sustained, can be made a priority. They do not set out clearly enough what church is *for* and what questions it must answer if mission is to be successful and evangelism to make any sense. They appear to assume that all that is somehow understood, or can be easily described using traditional phrases, without realizing that it is that very process which has emptied churches in the first place. That is not to say the descriptions of how churches will be organized, what kinds of unit and style of working will be appropriate and so on, are in themselves wrong. They simply start in the wrong place. Textual communities can be organized in a variety of ways. The important thing is to make sure that they can operate as textual communities first. However, it may be that we need to give more thought, as we judge the competing models, to those that will enable rather than hinder the exilic process.

Second, modern attempts at application of the theme of exile, particularly some of those deriving from America, which result in a church which has withdrawn from society, are deeply ironic. There are good reasons why, in some special cases, churches should from time to time withdraw and reflect in private. Dietrich Bonhoeffer provides one such rationale, and it may be that in the eyes of these American writers modern-day America provides such special circumstances. However, from a British perspective, exile involves the church in an even greater awareness of, reaction to, and relationship with, the context in which it is set. Israel's argument is not with Babylon. It is with God. It is through being in Babylon that the new things about God become known.

Third, it is wrong to suppose that the structure of existing churches is inadequate to enable the textual communities of which we have spoken to flourish, or that the buildings so associated with church communities are a barrier to mission. We do not need bulldozers, but rather human catalysts and enablers. Historic church buildings offer great examples of how theologically adventurous our forebears were, even in their architecture and internal ordering. Indeed Richard Giles, who has made an impassioned and well-argued plea to take church buildings seriously because of what they say about the communities who use them, believes that we are the first generation to divorce theology from architecture. Effectively that is because we have given up on theology. He is deprecating about those who 'attempt to address God in the language of today amidst the debris of yesterday's church and the preservationist constraints imposed by those who have no understanding of the Christian vocation'.[45] And the alterations that are made to the buildings or the language must be consistent with a vision of what the church is for and what that building is for. On the other hand, given that theological vision, the building can be a great embodiment of it. It is especially clear from Giles' examples that churches that embark on reordering have a strong sense of the importance of worship. The exilic church comes in all shapes, sizes and cultures. It does not have the one-size-fits-all conveniences of easy detection. Very traditional-looking churches can be textual. Many more modern-looking ones need not be.

Fourth, there are clear implications here for the training of ministers. The key stages in training need to be related to the need to read both the traditions of the church and the context of the ministry skilfully and perceptively; to be formed as a practical theologian; and to enable others to become theologians.

Fifth, if we take the exilic church as a useful metaphor or signal towards a style of church life, then some theological agendas will have to change. Just as the P theology reacted to what must have been a very successful D theology enabling people, as it did, to cope with sin; so we must not allow ourselves to think that only those successful-looking churches which major on sin have got it right. There are other issues, and indeed other ways of looking at sin.

Sixth, using the time of Exile, and its New Testament counterpart, to hold a mirror to contemporary church life helps us to see the extent of a culture of denial in our own churches. It is also helpful (and from my perspective, heartening) to reflect that it was those strong advocates of denial in Job who were guilty of the misrepresentation of God, even though they were a majority. They brought their God in their hand (Job 12:6). They had complete understanding of him and his systems. They knew how those systems operated, and were indeed themselves part of the mechanism. How many church groups today appear to have their God in their hand and to speak for him with complete confidence! How many churches operate systems of so-called pastoral care that amount to little more than persuading people to accept what Job denies! How many churches understand religion within a context of vindication that seems to suppose that the crucifixion never happened, or at the very least that the resurrection somehow emasculates it of any real significance! Using the Exile as a model forces us afresh to look at questions of suffering, justice, destiny and how evil is to be overcome in the end, and how life can be realistically bearable.

Seventh, this view gives us a pastoral basis for theology. Indeed it connects the two elements of giving careful attention to experience and context on the one hand with intelligent and reflective reading of tradition on the other. This is the extent to which the term 'parish' has proved useful in our study. Theology grows from pastoral situations, encounters and needs. It must have a local context and sense of place. The modern use of the term 'parish' provides that, as well as providing an appropriate setting for the articulation of theological responses. I have argued that the sense of alienation and juxtaposition implied by the derivation and early use of the term is no longer always appropriate.

The vision outlined here will not appeal to those who want to use the term exile in a different way.

In the first place, it will not appeal to those who want to use it to describe the church as having a cultural understanding distinct from that of post-modernism. That is to say, it will not appeal to those who believe that the church's main mark of identity in these times is that it holds to one truth and one story as a way of expressing meaning, in a world which increasingly finds lots of truths in many different ways. The question that is important for such a society is not: What is truth? but rather: What is truth for me, here and now? There is a real role here for the exilic church. In its suspicion of religious systems and mechanical theories of salvation, on the one hand, and its humble and cautious preparedness to listen to culture on the other, such a religious community may well be a home for those post-modern people who feel rendered homeless by many churches.

Secondly, it will not appeal to those whose reading of the exile traditions leads them to the point in the apocalyptic tradition where the community of faith is described as a small remnant who have kept the rules and traditions, and await the reward of vindication, and who believe that that is the most appropriate mode of church life today. 'Remnant', like 'Soldiers of Christ', is an ecclesiological title worked out in a particular setting using particular resources in response to particular experience. The exile form of church makes such theological work possible. It does not commit us to any one outcome. There may well be situations in the world today that call for a remnant style of church, but a) that should not in itself be equated with the exilic tradition, and b) I for one do not believe that ours is one of them.

Thirdly, it will not appeal to those for whom control is an important part of the theological agenda. That may include churches with rigid ministry patterns. But there is a far larger constituency of those who want to see something other than the individual community of faith as the guarantor of truth and creator of tradition, and they will be challenged by the view set out here.

Finally, it will not appeal to those who, as Dave Tomlinson describes in *The Post Evangelical,* want to erect an alternative Christian universe. He is dismissive of those who want to create Christian equivalents of every real life human institution. So, for example, there is Christian music, Christian holidays, Christian investments, Christian businesses, Christian printed tee-shirts. 'The Christian sub-culture has never known such a boom period in which "disinfected" versions of previously forbidden fruit abound.'[46] Neither will it speak to those for whom rejection by the

world is a comforting sign of success rather than a challenging mark of failure. Exile might be used to describe
both groups, but not in a biblical sense.

It *is* likely to appeal, and hopefully even to give new
heart, to those who want to have a faith and church life as
part of a 'normal' life lived within society on the same terms
as everyone else. Included among them would be those who
believe that the church is meant to help people to be truly
human rather than to help them to be religious, as both
Bonhoeffer and Auden might have put it. It will appeal to
those who want to be taken seriously by their church, and
have some place where serious things and significant things
can be both articulated and reflected on. It will appeal to
those who do not exactly feel totally at home in the world
of Babylon but who nevertheless recognize that they have
to live there for the time being. And it will appeal, hopefully,
to those who still have more questions than answers, but
whose faith in the 'bold nevertheless' still inspires them
(along with Habakkuk) to want to have some public place
to say:

> Though the fig tree does not blossom, and no fruit is on
> the vines; though the produce of the olive fails and the
> fields yield no food; though the flock is cut off from the
> fold and there is no herd in the stalls, yet I will rejoice in
> the Lord; I will exult in the God of my salvation.
> (Habakkuk 3:17f.)

Final Reflection

What difference has reading this book made to:

- Your understanding of what church is or might be?
- Your critical judgement of the church today?
- Your understanding of Bible texts about exile?
- Your personal commitment and faith?

Notes

1. David J. A. Clines, *Interested Parties*, Sheffield, Sheffield Academic Press, 1995, p. 34.
2. Walter Brueggemann, *Cadences of Home*, Louisville, Kentucky, WJK, 1997, p. 4.
3. C. C. Torrey, quoted by Daniel Smith-Christopher, *Biblical Theology in Exile*, Minneapolis, Augsburg Fortress Press, 2002, p. 30.
4. Smith-Christopher, *Biblical Theology*, p. 6.
5. A. van Selms, *Job: A Practical Commentary*, tr. John Vriend, Grand Rapids, Mich. Eerdmans, 1985.
6. Brueggemann, *Cadences*, p. 5.
7. Donald Gowan, *Eschatology in the Old Testament*, 2nd edn, Edinburgh, T & T Clark, 2002, p. 2.
8. Jürgen Moltmann, *The Crucified God: The Cross of Christ as the Foundation and Criticism of Christian Theology*, London, SCM Press, 1974, p. 17.
9. Walter Brueggemann, 'A Shattered Transcendence? Exile and Restoration', in Patrick D. Miller (ed.), *Old Testament Theology: Essays on Structure, Theme and Text*, Minneapolis, Fortress Press, 1992, pp. 183–203.
10. Stephen Neill, *The Interpretation of the New Testament 1861–1961*, Oxford, Oxford University Press, 1963, p. 343.
11. John Elliott, *A Home for the Homeless*, Minneapolis, Fortress Press, 1990.
12. Susan Thistlethwaite and George Cairns, *Beyond Theological Tourism*, Maryknoll, NY, Orbis, 1994.
13. Adrian Hastings (ed.), *The Oxford Companion to Christian Thought*, Oxford, Oxford University Press, 2000, p, 227.
14. Ralph Klein, *Israel in Exile: A Theological Interpretation*, Minneapolis, Fortress Press, 1979, p. 150.

15. Stanley Hauerwas and William H. Willimon, *Resident Aliens*, Nashville, Tenn., Abingdon Press, 1989.

16. Hauerwas and Willimon, *Resident Aliens*, p. 48.

17. Hauerwas and Willimon, *Resident Aliens*, p. 107.

18. William H. Willimon, Martin B. Copenhaver and Anthony B. Robinson, *Good News in Exile*, Grand Rapids, Mich., Eerdmans, 1999.

19. Walter Brueggemann, Preface to Willimon, Copenhaver and Robinson, *Good News*, p. x.

21. Brueggemann, *Cadences*, p. 2. Walter Brueggemann, Foreword to Smith-Christopher, *Biblical Theology*, p. vii.

22. See note 14.

23. Klein, *Israel in Exile*, p. 151.

24. Klein, *Israel in Exile*, p. 149.

25. J. Woodward and S. Pattison (eds), *The Blackwell Reader in Pastoral and Practical Theology*, Oxford, Blackwell, 2000, p. xiii.

26. Nicholas Bradbury, 'Ecclesiology and Pastoral Theology', in Woodward and Pattison (eds), *Blackwell Reader*, 174.

27. Brueggemann, *Cadences*, pp. 15–23.

28. Brueggemann, *Cadences*, p. 4.

29. Brueggemann, *Cadences*, pp. 12f.

30. N. Lohfink, *Theology of the Pentateuch*, trans. L. Maloney, Minneapolis, Fortress Press, 1994, p. 97.

31. Klein, *Israel in Exile*, p. 143.

32. Lohfink, *Pentateuch*, pp. 35–95.

33. Willliam J. Larkin, Jr, *Acts*, (IVP New Testament Commentary), Leicester, Intervarsity Press, 1995, p. 303.

34. Hans-Ruedi Weber, *Experiments with Bible Study*, Geneva, World Council of Churches, 1981, pp. 225ff.

35. John A. T. Robinson, *Jesus and His Coming*, London, SCM Press, 1957.

36. S. Croft, *Transforming Communities*, London, Darton, Longman & Todd, 2002, pp. 109–61.

37. Martin Stringer, *On the Perception of Worship: The Ethnography of Worship in Four Christian Congregations in Manchester*, Birmingham, University of Birmingham Press, 1999.

38. Walter Brueggemann, *The Message of the Psalms*, Minneapolis, Augsburg, 1984.

39. Brueggemann, *Message*, p. 25.

40. Brueggemann, *Message*, p. 51.

41. Brueggemann, *Message*, pp. 52ff.

42. Bueggemann, *Message*, p. 124.

43. Michael Goulder, *The Psalms of the Return: Book Five, Pss. 107–150*, Sheffield: Sheffield Academic Press, 1998.

44. Reardon, Martin, *What on Earth Is the Church For?: A Study Course for Lent '86*, prepared for the inter-church process 'Not Strangers but Pilgrims', London, British Council of Churches and the Catholic Truth Society, 1985.

45. Richard Giles, *Re-Pitching the Tent*, Norwich, Canterbury Press, 1999, p. 5.

46. Dave Tomlinson, *The Post Evangelical*, London, SPCK, 1997, p. 124.